Thicket P

Foundation to Dissolution

Colin Blanshard Withers

2022

Preface

Considerable work has been expended by academics and historians on the history of the great abbeys and monasteries that covered the English landscape since the Norman Conquest. However, the same cannot be said about the lesser religious houses, and even less so on nunneries.

However, in recent times some attention has fallen on even the most humble of these priories, and few were as humble as the Benedictine Priory of Thicket in the Ouse and Derwent area of the East Riding of Yorkshire, a sparsely populated area that was heavily wooded with low quality scrub and thickets and subject to frequent flooding.

Thicket Priory was founded before 1180, possibly as early as 1162, and survived until it was dissolved by Henry VIII in 1539. Thicket followed the Rule of St. Benedict, but also claimed to be of the Cistercian Order, which was disputed and led to a case before the Ecclesiastical Court of York. In order to understand the issues at the heart of this case the background to the Benedictines and Cistercians is briefly discussed in the opening chapter.

Most nunneries in England during the medieval period were poor, and this was the case in the East Riding of Yorkshire, where none came close to the £200 per annum threshold to avoid the first wave of Dissolutions. Thicket was middling in income, having a clear annual value of under £21 per annum.

It is hoped that this monograph will add to the corpus of histories of these smaller religious houses.

Bishop's Stortford, October, 2022

Acknowledgements

My grateful thanks are due to the archivists and staff of The National Archives (TNA), who have been unstinting in their support and suggestions. My thanks are also due to Bruce Westcott and Dr. Matthew Tompkins of Leicester University for their help with the more tricky idiosyncrasies of medieval Latin and administrative practice. Thanks are also due to the staff of the Borthwick Institute for Archives at the University of York, for their help with the medieval registers of the archbishops of York; the staff of the Department of Manuscripts in the British Library; and all the staff of the various archives and libraries throughout Yorkshire who helped in locating and providing digital copies of many unpublished manuscripts.

My thanks must also go to the last remaining member of the Dunnington-Jefferson family who once lived at Thicket Priory, Rosemary Nicolette Dunnington-Jefferson (Nicky to her friends), who proof-read the entire text and provided many corrections and observations.

Last, but not least, my thanks are due to Bruce Corrie, the current owner of the reborn Thicket Priory whose support has been most encouraging.

Contents

Abbreviations

BI	The Borthwick Institute for Archives, University of York
BIHR	Bulletin of the Institute of Historical Research
BP	Borthwick Papers
BTC	Borthwick Texts and Calendars
BTS	Borthwick Texts and Studies
CP	The Complete Peerage
CYS	Canterbury and York Society
EHR	English Historical Review
EYC	Early Yorkshire Charters
EYF	Early Yorkshire Families
HMC	Historical Manuscripts Commission
HMSO	His/Her Majesty's Stationery Office
L&P	Letters and Papers, Henry VIII (see Bibliography)
PRS	Pipe Roll Society (Publications of)
TNA	The National Archives, Kew, London
VCH	Victoria County History
YAJ	Yorkshire Archaeological Journal

Bibliography and other Sources

All works producing two or more references in the text are included here. Works that produce a single reference in the text are quoted directly in the footnotes.

I. *Modern Works*

Ancient Deeds MAXWELL-LYTE, H. C., (ed.), *A Descriptive Catalogue of Ancient Deeds*, vol. 1, (HMSO, 1890)

Baildon's *Notes* BAILDON, William Paley, *Notes on the Religious and Secular Houses of Yorkshire*, 2 volumes, YASRS 17 and 81 (1895, 1931)

Burton, *Causes* BURTON, Janet, 'The Convent and the Community: Cause Papers as a Source for Monastic History', in Hoskin, Brooke, Dobson (eds.), *The Foundations of Medieval English Ecclesiastical History: Studies Presented to David Smith*, (2005)

Burton, *Nunneries* BURTON, Janet, *The Yorkshire Nunneries in the Twelfth and Thirteenth Centuries*, Borthwick Papers 56, (1979)

Burton, *Monasticon* BURTON, John, *Monasticon Eboracense and the Ecclesiastical History of Yorkshire*, (York, 1758)

Carpenter CARPENTER, David X., *The Cartulary of St. Leonard's Hospital, York*, 2 vol. set: YASRS vol. CLXIII, and BTS, 42, (2015)

Catholic Encyclopedia HERBERMANN, C. G., (ed.), *Catholic Encyclopedia*, 15 vols., (New York, 1907–1912)

Chartulary, *Fountains* LANCASTER, William T., *Abstracts of the charters and other documents contained in the chartulary of the Cistercian Abbey of Fountains in the West Riding of the County of York*, 2 vols., (1915)

Cheney   CHENEY, C. R., *Episcopal Visitation of Monasteries in the Thirteenth Century*, (Manchester University Press, 2nd Ed. 1983)

Clark   CLARK, James G., (ed.), *The Religious Orders in Pre-Reformation England*, (The Boydell Press, 2002)

Coredon   COREDON, Christopher, *A Dictionary of Medieval Terms & Phrases*, (2007)

Cross, *Nuns*   CROSS, Claire, *Monks, Friars and Nuns in Sixteenth Century Yorkshire,* YASRS 149, (2000)

Cross, *Medieval*   CROSS, Claire, *The End of Medieval Monasticism in the East Riding of Yorkshire*, East Yorks Local History Series, No. 87, (1993)

Dickens   DICKENS, A.G., *Reformation Studies*, (London, 1982)

Dugdale,   DUGDALE, Sir William, (A New Edition by Caley, Ellis
Monasticon   and Bandinel), *Monasticon Anglicanum*, 6 vols., (1846–1849)

Encyclopædia   CHISHOLM, Hugh, (ed.), *Encyclopædia Britannica*, (11th
Britannica   ed., Cambridge University Press, 1911)

EYC   FARRER, William (first 3 vols.), CLAY, Charles Travis (vols. 4–12), *Early Yorkshire Charters*, 12 vols., (1914–1965)

EYF   CLAY, Charles and GREENWAY, Diana E., *Early Yorkshire Families* (Cambridge University Press, 2013)

Feudal Aids   THE DEPUTY KEEPER OF THE RECORDS, *Inquisitions and assessments relating to feudal aids, with other analogous documents preserved in the Public Record Office A.D. 1284–1431*, vol. VI, York and Additions, (1920)

Foster	FOSTER, Joseph, (ed.), *The visitation of Yorkshire, made in the years 1584–85: to which is added the subsequent visitation made in 1612, by Richard St. George, Norry King of Arms*, Privately Printed, (London, 1875)
France	FRANCE, James, *Separate but Equal: Cistercian Lay Brothers 1120–1350*, Cistercian Studies Series: 246, (2012)
Fryde	FRYDE, E. B., *Handbook of British Chronology*, 3rd Edition (Royal Historical Society, Cambridge University Press, 1986)
Helmholz	HELMOLZ, R. H., *The Oxford History of the Laws of England: Volume I: The Canon Law and Ecclesiastical Jurisdiction from 597 to the 1640s*, (Oxford University Press, 2004)
Hoffman	HOFFMAN, Richard C., 'A brief history of aquatic resource use in medieval Europe', in *Helgoland Marine Research*, vol. 59, Issue 1, (2005)
Hoyle	HOYLE, R. W., *The Pilgrimage of Grace and the Politics of the 1530s*, (Oxford University Press, 2001)
Kirkby's Inquest	SKAIFE, Robert H., *The survey of the County of York taken by John de Kirkby, commonly called Kirkby's Inquest; also inquisitions of knights' fees, the Nomina villarum for Yorkshire, and an appendix of illustrative documents*, Surtees Society, vol. XLIX, (1867)
Knowles	KNOWLES, Dom. David, *The Religious Orders in England*, (Cambridge University Press, 1950)
Knowles & Smith	KNOWLES, David; SMITH, David M., *The Heads of Religious Houses: England and Wales*, III. 1377–1540 (London, 2011)

L&P | BREWER, GAIRDNER and BRODIE, (eds.), *Letters and Papers, Foreign and Domestic, of the Reign of Henry VIII*, (in 21 volumes, 1862–1910)

McDonnell | MCDONNELL, J., *Inland Fisheries in Medieval Yorkshire*, Borthwick Papers 60, (1981)

Memorials, Fountains | FOWLER, J. T., (ed.), *Memorials of the Abbey of St. Mary of Fountains, vol. III, Bursars' Books, 1456–1459, and Memorandum Book of Thomas Swynton, 1446–1458*, Surtees Society vol. CXXX, (1918)

Purvis | PURVIS, J. S., (ed.), 'A Selection of Monastic Rentals and Dissolution Papers', in *Miscellanea III*, YASRS 80, (1931)

RC, *Chartarum* | RECORD COMMISSIONERS, *Rotuli Chartarum in Turri Londinensi Asservati*, (London, 1837)

Reg.Corbridge | BROWN, William, (ed.), *The Register of Thomas of Corbridge: Lord Archbishop of York 1300–1304*, 2 vols., Surtees Society, vols. 138, 141, (1925–1928)

Reg.Greenfield | BROWN, William, (ed.), *The Register of William Greenfield, Lord Archbishop of York, 1306–1315*, 5 vols., Surtees Society, vols. 145, 149, 151, 152, 153, (1931–1940)

Reg.Romeyn | BROWN, William, (ed.), *The Register of John Le Romeyn, Lord Archbishop of York, 1286–1296*, 2 vols., Surtees Society, vols. 123, 128, (1913–1917)

Reg.Rotherham | BARKER, E. E., (ed.), *The Register of Thomas Rotherham, Archbishop of York, 1480–1500*, vol. 1, Canterbury and York Society, vol. 69, (1976)

Reg.Melton | HILL, ROBINSON, BROCKLESBY, TIMMINS, (eds.), *The Register of William Melton, Archbishop of York, 1317–1340*, 6 vols., Canterbury and York Society, vols. 70, 71, 76, 85, 93, 101, (1977–2011)

Reg.Scrope	SWANSON, R. N., (ed.), *A Calendar of the Register of Richard Scrope, Archbishop of York, 1397*, 2 vols., BTC 8, 11, (1981–1985)
Reg.Waldby	SMITH, D. M., (ed.), *A Calendar of the Register of Robert Waldby, Archbishop of York, 1397*, BTC 2, (1974)
Roger of Howden	STUBBS, William, (ed.), *Chronica Magistri Rogeri de Houedene*, Rolls Series, 4 vols., (London 1868–1871)
Skaife	SKAIFE, Robert H., *The Register of the Guild of Corpus Christi in the City of York*, Surtees Society, vol. LVII, (London, 1871)
Swanson	SWANSON, Robert Norman, *A Calendar of the Register of Richard Scrope, Archbishop of York, 1398–1405*, 2 vols., Borthwick Texts and Calendars, vols. 8, 11, (1981, 1985)
Taxatio	DENT, Jeff, et al., *Taxatio*. (HRI Online, Sheffield, 2014). Available at: http://www.hrionline.ac.uk/taxatio
Testamenta Eboracensia	RAINE, James, (ed.), *Testamenta Eboracensia*, Surtees Society, vols. 4, 30, 45, 53, (London, 1836–1869)
Tobin	TOBIN, Stephen, *The Cistercians: Monks and Monasteries in Europe*, (1995)
Turner	TURNER, William H., (ed.), *Calendar of Charters and Rolls Preserved in the Bodleian Library*, (London, 1878)
Valor Ecclesiasticus	RECORD COMMISSIONERS, *Valor Ecclesiasticus, Temp. Henr. VIII, Auctoritate Regia, Institutus*, vol. 5, Diocese of York, Chester, Carlisle, Durham, (1826)
VCH, *General*	PAGE, William, (ed.), *A History of the County of York*, vol. III, *Religious Houses*, (London, 1974)

VCH, *East*	ALLISON, K. J., (ed.), *A History of the County of York, East Riding*: vol. 3, *Ouse and Derwent Wapentake, and Part of Harthill Wapentake*, (London, 1976)
Waites	WAITES, Brian, 'The Monasteries of North-East Yorkshire and the Medieval Wool Trade', in *Yorkshire Archaeological Journal*, vol. 52, (1980)
Woodward	WOODWARD, G. W. O., 'The Exemption from Suppression of Certain Yorkshire Priories', in *The English Historical Review*, no. CCC, (July 1961)

II. Published Public Records

CChR	*Calendar of the Charter Rolls preserved in the Public Record Office.* (London: HMSO, 1903–1927)
CCR	*Calendar of the Close Rolls preserved in the Public Record Office.* (London: HMSO, 1892–1963)
CFR	*Calendar of Fine Rolls preserved in the Public Record Office.* (London: HMSO, 1911–1962)
CIM	*Calendar of Inquisitions Miscellaneous (Chancery) preserved in the Public Record Office.* (London: HMSO, 1916–present)
CIPM	*Calendar of Inquisitions Post-Mortem and other Analogous Documents preserved in the Public Record Office.* (London: HMSO, 1904–present)
CLR	*Calendar of the Liberate Rolls*, 6 vols., 1226–1267. (London: HMSO, 1916–1964)
CPR	*Calendar of the Patent Rolls preserved in the Public Record Office.* (London: HMSO, 1891–1986)

Hen. III Project	*Henry III Fine Rolls Project*, online resource at: https://finerollshenry3.org.uk/home.html
L&P	Letters and Papers, Foreign and Domestic, of the Reign of Henry VIII
PRS	Publications of the Pipe Roll Society, (for full list see their website, http://www.piperollsociety.co.uk/page4.htm)
YASRS	Yorkshire Archaeological Society, Record Series, (for full list see their website, https://www.yas.org.uk/Portals/0/Documents/YAHSRS%20volumes.pdf?ver=2017-12-29-142749-663

III. Unprinted Public Records and Manuscripts

The National Archives

E 179	Lay Subsidies
SC 1	Ancient Correspondence
SC 6	Monastic Possessions of the Dissolved Religious Houses
SC 8	Ancient Petitions

Borthwick Institute For Archives, University of York

CP.F.221	Thicket Priory v. Ellerton Priory: tithes
YWT/5/52/1/3/3	Purchase of Thicket Priory

British Library

Cotton Tiberius C. XII	Cartulary of Fountains, vol. i, A–C

Add MSS 37779   Cartulary of Fountains, vol. iii, K–M

Leeds, West Yorkshire Archive Service
150/5385   Cartulary of Fountains, vol. ii, D–I

Manchester, The John Rylands University Library
Lat. 224   Cartulary of Fountains, vol. v, Q–Z

Note: The Cartulary of Fountains Abbey is in five volumes, all dispersed as above, but the whereabouts of volume iv, N–P, is currently unknown

Hull History Centre
U DDJ   Papers of the Dunnington-Jefferson Family of
                                 Thicket Priory

U DX55   Papers of the Aske Family of Aughton

CHAPTER 1
The Benedictines
St. Benedict – St. Scholastica – Expansion in Europe – Arrival in England –
Destroyed by the Danes – Reappearance in Yorkshire following the Norman
Conquest – The Cistercians

Benedict of Nursia (A.D. 480–547) studied in Rome from an early age, but was so disillusioned by the immorality he found there, that at the age of fourteen he gave up his studies and lived an hermitic life in a cave in Subiaco around fifty miles east of Rome. His great piety attracted followers and he founded several communities for monks near Rome, before establishing an Abbey at Monte Cassino in the mountains of southern Italy.[1]

While at the Abbey he wrote his famous Rule, which set out in seventy-three simple chapters his principles for leading a monastic life. The Rule covered: how to live a Christocentric life; how to administer a monastery efficiently; how to behave obediently and humbly (and what to do with inmates who were refractory); how to manage the work of God (the *Opus Dei* of the Catholic church); and the management of a monastery.[2]

Benedict was influenced in writing his Rule by the works of the monk Johan Cassian (John the Ascetic) and by the *Regula Magistri* (Rule of the Master), but was more reasonable and balanced, making it attractive to Christian communities, and its popularity spread. Around A.D. 594 Pope Gregory the Great praised the Rule, and Benedict, which further increased the popularity of both. Communities of Benedictines sprang up rapidly throughout Europe, and in A.D. 816/17 an important synod declared that Benedict's Rule was binding for all monks.[3]

Scholastica (c. 480–1543) was the sister of Benedict of Nursia, and according to one tradition was the twin sister of Benedict. Scholastica established a community of consecrated virgins close to Monte Cassino which has been traditionally considered the first convent of Benedictine nuns.[4]

The Benedictines were never an 'order' in the normal sense of the word.

---

[1] Ford, Hugh. 'St. Benedict of Norcia' in *Catholic Encyclopedia*, vol. 2
[2] *ibid.*
[3] *ibid.*
[4] https://www.osb.org//gen/scholastica.html

Rather, it was a loose confederation of independent religious houses. They were typically governed by an abbot or prior (abbess or prioress), and modelled on the 'family', with the abbot or prior being the 'father' and the monks 'brothers', and similarly the abbess or prioress being the 'mother' and the nuns 'sisters'. They were easily distinguished from other monks due to their black habits, which led them to be called the Black Monks.[5]

In England, Augustine of Canterbury and his monks established the first English Benedictine monastery at Canterbury soon after their arrival in the late sixth century, and the Benedictine Rule spread rapidly. In the North of England it was adopted in most of the monasteries that had been founded by the Celtic missionaries, beginning with Whitby in A.D. 657.[6]

However, all the monasteries in the North were destroyed during the Danish invasions of the ninth and tenth centuries, and this desolation continued until the Danes were themselves supplanted by the Normans following the Conquest. Burton wrote: 'Yorkshire in 1066 could truly be called a "monastic wilderness"; indeed apart from a few quasi-religious settlements such as that which may have existed at the church of Holy Trinity, York, there was a complete absence of recognizable monastic life north of the river Trent'.[7]

Following the establishment of Selby Abbey in 1069, and Whitby c. 1078, the Benedictines once again began to flourish. By 1140 the number of religious houses in Yorkshire rose to around twenty, and included two, possibly three, nunneries. In the second half of the twelfth century twelve more monasteries were founded, but over twenty nunneries. Unfortunately, the chronology of the foundation of these early nunneries is problematic due to a lack of documentary evidence, and only one nunnery, that of Nunkeeling, is known to have had a cartulary.

The Benedictine nunneries established in Yorkshire in the thirteenth century, and early fourteenth century, with approximate dates of foundation, were: York, St Clement's, (1125x1133); Nunkeeling, (1143x1153); Wilberfoss, (1147x1153); Nun Monkton, (1147x1153); Arden, (1147x1169); Marrick, (1154x1158); Yedingham, (*ante* 1158); Thicket, (*ante* 1180);

[5] Alston, Cyprian (1907). 'Benedictine Order' in *Catholic Encyclopedia*. vol. 2
6 *ibid.*
7 Burton, *Nunneries*, p. 5

Nunburnholme, (*ante* 1188); Foukeholme, (*ante* 1226, dissolved 1308–12).[8]

At this point it is necessary, for reasons that will be made clear in the External Community chapter, to briefly discuss the Cistercian Order.

The name Cistercian is derived from *Cistercium* (the Latin for Cîteaux, near Dijon) in eastern France, where the Order branched off from the Benedictines in 1098 after a group of monks from Molesme founded Cîteaux Abbey.

The Cistercians still followed the Rule of Benedict, but rejected the developments the Benedictines had undergone, and tried to go back to the Rule as it had been during Saint Benedict's lifetime. They were readily distinguishable from the original Benedictines due to their undyed woollen habits, which led them to be called the White Monks.

The Order grew in popularity and by the end of the twelfth century had spread throughout Europe, reaching England in 1128, when Waverley Abbey was founded in Surrey. In Yorkshire, Rievaulx Abbey was founded in 1131, Fountains Abbey in 1132, and Meaux in 1151.[9]

The Cistercians employed their own manual labour to obtain self-sufficiency. They accepted gifts of land on which to build their houses, farm sheep for wool and grow food, quarry stone and retrieve timber for building and repairs. However, initially at least, they would accept only undeveloped land.

In 1132, in return for the support of the Cistercians during the Great Schism, Pope Innocent II, granted the Order freedom from the paying of tithes from land they cultivated themselves.[10] This led to some Benedictine nunneries claiming to be Cistercian simply to avoid paying tithes, and the abbot of Cîteaux complained directly about this practice.[11]

---

[8] Burton, *Nunneries*, Appendix I, pp. 38–43

[9] 'Cistercians', in Encyclopædia Britannica

[10] France, p. 303

[11] Burton, *Causes*, p. 69

CHAPTER 2

Foundation of Thicket Priory

Foundation Grants – Later Grants – Other Property Interests –
Testamentary Bequests and Burials

Before the foundation of Thicket Priory is discussed certain clarifications need to be made concerning the persons mentioned. It has been held that the founder of Thicket Priory was Roger son of Roger, and that this man was in fact Roger Hay. The origin of this identification were the works of Farrer,[12] and Clay and Greenway.[13] Farrer provided the following:

'Robert Fossard apparently enfeoffed Roger, father of Roger, of these 6 carucates [manor of Aughton], 4 in Everthorpe, 4 in North Cave, and 6 in Goodmanham to hold for the service of one knight. This was one of the 2 fees held in 1166 by Roger, son of Roger. He was succeeded by Thomas Hay, apparently his son and heir, and presumably husband of Emma Hay, daughter of Roger, son of Alured. Thomas Hay I confirmed a gift made to the hospital of St. Peter, York, by the younger Roger, his father-in-law, as given above.'[14]

The use of 'apparently' and 'presumably' show that Farrer was being cautious in the absence of proof. However, Clay and Greenway, summarising and expanding Farrer, removed the caution, and stated the following as fact:

'In 1166 Roger son of Roger held 2 knights' fees of William Fossard, consisting of land in Huggate, North Cave, Everthorpe (par. N. Cave), Aughton and Laytham (par. Aughton). He was the founder of Thicket Priory, and was succeeded by his son Thomas, who confirmed gifts in North Cave made by his father Roger *Hay*[15] to St. Peter's hospital, c. 1175–1188. Thomas married Emma daughter and heir of Roger son of Alvred, and died before Michaelmas 1190, when Thomas son of Thomas son of Roger paid 100s. for a recognition of the death of his father respecting land in Aughton and Goodmanham, of which Roger de Hay was deforcing him.' A note on this text states that the last named Roger de Hay 'has not been identified; he may have

---

[12] EYC

[13] EYF

[14] EYC, vol. ii, p. 423

[15] My italics

been a younger brother of Thomas the elder.'[16] The preceding text leads to the following (inaccurate) pedigree:

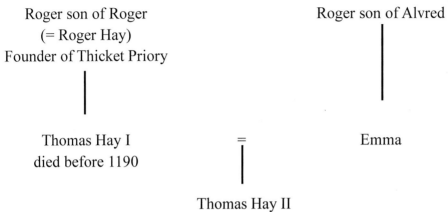

Roger son of Roger   Roger son of Alvred
(= Roger Hay)
Founder of Thicket Priory

Thomas Hay I   =   Emma
died before 1190

Thomas Hay II

It was Carpenter who demonstrated that the above pedigree was in error on several points, and Farrer had been right to be cautious. Roger son of Roger was not identical with Roger Hay. Roger son of Roger did not have a son named Thomas, and, in fact, died without issue, and Emma did not marry Thomas Hay, but was sister to Roger and Thomas, sons of Roger, and married the Roger de Hay that Clay and Greenway were unable to identify.

Roger de Hay of North Cave was identical with Roger de Hay of Hunston (near Chichester) and sheriff of Sussex 1163–1170. He lived mainly on his Sussex estates, explaining why he left little mark in Yorkshire,[17] and died between 1190 and 1196. Carpenter also showed that Emma was the daughter of Roger, son of Alured, but crucially the heir of her brother, Roger, son of Roger.[18] Carpenter corrected these errors and provided a revised pedigree. The following notes on the foundation and endowments of Thicket Priory should therefore be used with reference to the following revised pedigree.

---

[16] EYF, pp. 40–41

[17] Although Roger was listed in *Kirkby's Inquest* (The Return of Knights' Fees in 1166) which showed that Roger, son of Roger "de Haye" held Aughton under William Fossard. Roger's son and heir, Thomas Haye, succeeded to the manor. For a detailed account of the descent of Aughton through the Haye family, see EYC, vol. ii, page 423

[18] Carpenter, vol. 2, pp. 677–686

Revised Pedigree of the Founders of Thicket Priory

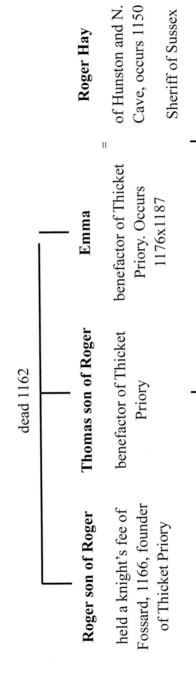

Roger son of Alured

dead 1162

Roger son of Roger

held a knight's fee of
Fossard, 1166, founder
of Thicket Priory

Thomas son of Roger

benefactor of Thicket
Priory

Emma

benefactor of Thicket
Priory. Occurs
1176x1187

=

Roger Hay

of Hunston and N.
Cave, occurs 1150

Sheriff of Sussex

Thomas son of Thomas son of Roger

Occurs 1190

Thomas Hay

Occurs 1176x1187

just a note…

PLAND PUTTE
MIXTIXIS

SICTCH Basic

Prairis pnp

We know that Thicket was founded as early as the reign of Richard I,[19] and probably during the reign of Henry II.[20] However, a charter of confirmation of King John does exist, dated 27 February, in the fifth year of his reign, (1203–4), which lists the first seven benefactors:

Carta Regis Johannis
[Cart. 5 Johannis, m. 12, n. 98. Pat. 13 Edw. I. m. 20.]

Johannes Dei gratia, &c. Sciatis nos intuitu Dei et pro salute animæ nostræ et animarum antecessorum et successorum concessisse et præsenti carta nostra confirmasse Deo et ecclesiæ sanctæ Mariæ de Thikeheved et monialibus Ibidem Deo servientibus rationabiles donationes eis factas inferius scriptas; scilicet de dono Rogeri fil. Rogeri locum qui dicitur Tikeheved et iiij. bovatas terræ cum pertinentiis in Cottungwich. De dono Thomæ fil. Rogeri dimid. carucatam terræ cum pertinen. in eadem villa. De dono Picot unam bovatam terræ cum pertinentiis in eadem villa. De dono et concessione Gaufridi de Ficelingham et Hugonis de Buleton essartum quoddam de wasto nostro. De dono Rogeri filii Rogeri unam bovatam terræ cum pertinentiis in Gudemundeham. De dono Emmæ sororis ejusdem Rogeri filii Rogeri unam bovatam terræ cum pertinentiis in eadem villa. De dono Gaufridi de Ficelingham duas bovatas terræ cum pertinentiis in Coldric. De dono Hugonis de Boulton duas bovatas terræ cum pertinentiis in eadem villa. De dono Emmæ de Diholton unam bovatam terræ cum pertimentiis in eadem villa. Quare volo, &c. Testibus domino G. archiepiscopo Eborac. Ph. Dunelm. episcopo. G. fil. Petri, &c. Rob. filio Rogeri. Hugone de Nevill. Datum per manum S. præpositi Beverlaci et Wellensis archidiaconi, apud Eboracum, vicesimo septimo die Februarii, anno, &c. quinto.[21]

John by the grace of God, etc. Know that in consideration of God and for the salvation of our soul and that of our ancestors and successors and by our charter at hand have confirmed to God and the church of St.

---

[19] The charter of Hugh of Bolton, printed below, mentions the waste (land) of King Richard
[20] See the notes to Picot, one of the benefactors of Thicket, printed below
[21] Dugdale, *Monasticon*, vol. iv, pp. 385–386; RC, *Chartarum*, p. 120

Mary Thickhead and the nuns serving God in the same place the grants [in due form] made as written below; namely of the gift of Roger son of Roger the place called Thickhead and four oxgangs of land with the appurtenances belonging in Cottingwith. The gift of Thomas son of Roger half a carucate of land with the appurtenances belonging in the same township. The gift of Picot one oxgang of land with the appurtenances belonging in the same township. The gift and grant of Geoffrey of Ficelingham [Fitling][22] and Hugh of Bolton essart of land of our [the king's] waste. The gift of Roger son of Roger one oxgang of land with the appurtenances belonging in Goodmanham. The gift of Emma sister of the same Roger son of Roger, one oxgang of land with the appurtenances belonging in the same township. The gift of Geoffrey of Ficelingham two oxgangs of land with the appurtenances belonging in Queldrick [Wheldrake]. The gift of Hugh of Bolton two oxgangs of land with the appurtenances belonging in the same township. The gift of Emma of Diholton one oxgang of land with the appurtenances belonging in the same township.

Why I, etc. Witnesses: lord Geoffrey Archbishop of York; Philip, Bishop of Durham; G. son of Peter, etc; Robert son of Roger; Hugh de Nevill. Given by hand, Simon, provost of Beverley and archdeacon of Wells, at York.

This confirmation charter gives no clue as to the dates of the original grants, but one later charter does refer to a grant made during the reign of Richard I, 1189x1199, and there are clues to an even earlier date. Another charter gives a clue as to the identity of possibly the first prioress of Thicket, Sibilla. These later charters were printed in their original Latin by Dugdale,[23] and are reproduced here, with their English translation:

Carta Emmae Hai
[Ex ipso autog, penes Ric. Robinson de Thikhed ar. anno 1652.]

OMNIBUS sanctae matris ecclesiae filiis ego Emma Hai salutem. Sciatis me et haeredes meos concessisse et hac praesenti carta confirmasse Deo et sanctae Mariae de Thiched et sanctimonialibus

---

[22] See notes under Geoffrey de Fitling below
[23] Dugdale, *Monasticon*, vol. iv, pp. 384–388

ibidem Deo servientibus unambovatam terrae in Cotingwit quam Pigot et haeredes sui praedictis sanctimonialibus dederunt, et unum toftum in Crossum, ita liberê et quietè de me et haeredibus meis, sicut praedictus Pigot et haeredes sui praedictis sanctimonialibus carta sua confirmaverunt. His testibus, Rad. Salvage, Willielmo de Murrers, Hamone de Skipwic, Hugone de Boulton, Willi elmo filio Petri, Willielmo Hai, Willielmo de Belebia, et multis aliis.

To all the daughters of the church of Saint Mary, I, Emma Hay, greetings. Know that me and my heirs by this present charter have granted to God and Saint Mary of Thickhead and the nuns there serving one oxgang of land that Pigot and his heirs gave to the said nuns, and one toft in Crossom, free and exempt from me and my heirs, as the aforesaid Pigot and his heirs confirmed to the said nuns by his charter.

Carta Hugonis de Booltun
[ibid.]

SCIANT omnes, tam praesentes quam futuri, quod ego Hugo de Boolton et Cecilia uxor mea, concessu haeredum nostrorum, dedimus et concessimus, et hac praesenti carta nostra confirmavimus, Deo et sanctae Mariae de Thicheved, et monialibus *Ibidem* Deo servientibus, in puram et per petuam elemosinam, cum Isonda filia nostra totam partem nostram in castellaria et balliva de Queldric, cum omnibus pertinentiis, et duas acras terrae extra ballivam, unde capita extendunt se versus mariscum; et unam acram terrae; simi liter toftum unum juxta toftum Willielmi Muns; et que relam quam habui apud praedictam domum de terra, scilicet infra clausturam ejusdem domus, scilicet de wasto domini regis Ricardi, quietam clamavimus. Has praenominatas terras praedictae moniales liberê et quietè, pacifice et ho norifice, possidebunt, cum communi pastura, et omnibus aisiamentis, cum libero introitu et exitu et omnibus liber tatibus ejusdem villae pertinentibus. Hiis testibus, Odone capellano, Johanne de Birkin, Willielmo Aguillun, Willielmo de Murrers, Galfrido de Fiteling, Ricardo de Averenches, Hamundo de Duffeld, Gerardo clerico, Petro de Auvers, et multis aliis.

Let all persons, both now and in future, that I Hugh Bolton Hugh and Cecily my wife, and our heirs, have given and granted and by this present charter confirmed, to God and St Mary of Thicheved and the nuns there serving God, in pure and perpetual alms, with our daughter, Isonda, the whole of our part of the bailiwick of the castle in Queldric, with all its appurtenances, and outside of the bailiwick the two acres of land, extending towards the marsh; and an acre of land; similarly a toft next to the toft of William Muns; and the suit which he had at the said house and ground, namely within the boundaries of the toft, namely the waste of King Richard, quietly. The above-mentioned lands, the nuns aforesaid to take possession of, freely, quietly, peaceably, and honorably, with common pasture, with all easements and free entry and exit of the same town, and pertaining to all the holy sisters. These witnesses: Odone the chaplain; John of Birkin; William Aguillun; William of Murrers; Geoffrey of Fiteling; Richard de Averenches; Hamo of Duffield; Gerard the clerk; Peter of Auvers, and many others.

Taking the above gifts in order:

Roger, son of Roger

The first name in the charter of confirmation is without question the name of the founder, and his foundation grant, which consisted of two pieces of land. The land in 'Tikeheved' was almost certainly wild and uncultivated. If cultivated it was usual to give it as so many oxgangs (or bovates), *i.e.* land that could be ploughed. The name 'Tikeheved' suggests it was land covered in thicket, usually of alder, hazel or willow, which is still quite common in the marshy areas of the Ouse and Derwent area today, and situated on a head, or loop in the River Derwent. The amount of land was not given at this stage but later deeds, after it had been cleared of the thicket, confirmed that it amounted to ten oxgangs. Of course, the nuns would have little income from such land; at best small amounts from the sale of withies as the land was being cleared. They therefore needed some land that they could farm or lease quickly so they could have an immediate income, and this was provided by the second part of the grant, that of four oxgangs of land in West Cottingwith. But four oxgangs would not be enough to support even the smallest of convents, so it is almost certain that the second grant in the charter of confirmation was made at the same time. The charter of confirmation also refers to a separate grant by Roger son of Roger of one oxgang in Goodmanham.

Thicket Priory was dedicated to the Virgin Mary, as was common in nunneries, and in all probability the dedication was decided at its foundation.

Thomas son of Roger

Brother to Roger son of Roger, gave half a carucate of land (equal to four oxgangs) in West Cottingwith,[24] By 1190 Thomas son of Roger had died, as in that year Thomas, son of Thomas son of Roger, paid 100s. for entry into his father's lands in Aughton and Goodmanham of which Roger[25] [presumably Roger de Hay] was disseising him. Thomas son of Thomas did not live long after, and had died by 1196.

Picot (Pigot)

Picot held land in West Cottingwith, and in the charter of confirmation he granted one oxgang of land there. In the later charter of Emma Hay she confirmed Picot's gift (spelt Pigot in the charter of Emma) and added that his original charter also included one toft in Crossom. This confirmation by Emma Hay shows that Picot held the land of Emma, and was her tenant. As Emma was the heir of Roger son of Roger it is almost certain that Picot held the land under Roger son of Roger in the earlier charter of confirmation. This Picot was probably Picot de Lascelles of Escrick,[26] and if confirmed would place the foundation of Thicket Priory during the reign of Henry II. Picot's son, Roger de Lascelles would grant further land to Thicket Priory.

---

[24] A carucate was accepted as being eight oxgangs in this part of Yorkshire at this time, so the gift was of four oxgangs and was the amount of land that could be ploughed by a team of eight oxen in a season. The reason why the land was referred to as half a carucate, rather than four oxgangs, was that a carucate had feudal services attached to it that oxgangs did not. Also, acreage did not come into it, as the amount that could be ploughed by an oxen, or a team of eight oxen, varied with soil quality, rocky as opposed to loam, marshy as opposed to dry, etc.

[25] Presumably this Roger was Roger Hay. He probably came into the possession of the lands during the minority of Thomas son of Thomas son of Roger

[26] Escrick borders both Wheldrake and Thorganby. Between 1100 and 1145 the two main estates in Escrick, each consisting of four carucates, came into the hands of St. Mary's Abbey, York. The abbey in turn granted six carucates to Picot de Lascelles between 1145 and 1161, and the remaining two carucates to Picot's son, Roger de Lascelles, between 1197 and 1219, (VCH, *East*, pp. 17–28). See the pedigree of this Lascelles family in EYC, vol. v, p. 184. Picot died before Michaelmas 1179, when Roger his son was under age, and who was still under age at Michaelmas 1182 (EYC , vol. iv, p. 134). Further notes on this line of the Lascelles family can be found in *Complete Peerage*, vol. 7, (London 1929), pp. 444–445

Geoffrey de Fitling (Fitelingham, Ficelingham) and Hugh de Bolton[27]

Geoffrey de Fitling and Hugh de Bolton married the two daughters and heiresses of Thomas Darel of Wheldrake, Beatrice and Cecilly, respectively. Thomas Darel held Wheldrake under the Percys in 1166 and his holding passed to his daughters. Geoffrey de Fitling's son, also a Geoffrey, took the name Darel, and was the ancestor of the subsequent Darels of Wheldrake.[28] In the charter of confirmation Geoffrey and Hugh granted an essart[29] of land out of the king's waste. They also both granted two oxgangs each in Wheldrake.

In addition, by a separate charter, Hugh, along with his wife Cecily and their daughter Isonda granted the whole of their part of the bailiwick of the castle in Queldric [Wheldrake],[30] and two acres of land outside of the bailiwick and an acre of land, and a toft next to the toft of William Muns, and the suit which he had at the said house and ground, *i.e.* within the boundaries of the toft, namely the waste [land] of King Richard. This mention of the waste [land] of King Richard dates the suit to his reign, 1189x1199, but the charter of Hugh, Cecily and Isonda must be later, probably *c.* 1200–1201.[31]

Emma, sister of Roger son of Roger

In the confirmation charter, Emma, sister to Roger son of Roger, had given an oxgang of land to the priory in Goodmanham. At the time of the

---

[27] The confirmation charter of King John reads 'Fitelingh', which Dodsworth or Dugdale may have misread as 'Ficelingh', as the 't' and the 'c' are similar, but it was read correctly by Farrer. There is no such place as Ficelingham or Ficeling, in Yorkshire or elsewhere, but Fiteling, or Fitling does exist. It is a hamlet in the East Riding in the parish of Humbleton. There are several references to the family of 'de Fitling' in EYC, vols. i–iii, and in particular vol. xi

[28] EYC, vol. xi, *The Percy Fee*, pp. 186–192. *Vide* the pedigree of the family, p. 188

[29] Essart, a form of assart, land recovered from forest for cultivation. This is probably the thicket type of forestry common in the marshy areas of the Ouse and Derwent. Another name for land recovered in this way is ridding, and Ridding is a common placename and fieldname in the lands either side of the River Derwent

[30] This 'castle of Wheldrake' is discussed further under *Richard Malbis (Mallebisse)*

[31] *ibid.*

confirmation charter all of the descendants of Roger son of Alured had died: Roger son of Roger; Thomas son of Roger; and his son Thomas; and Emma. As both of her brothers and her nephew Thomas, son of Thomas son of Roger had predeceased Emma she was left as the sole heir to her father's lands, which in turn descended to the de Hay family by her marriage to Roger de Hay.

Following her marriage, now as Emma Hay, she confirmed the grant to Thicket Priory made by Picot in West Cottingwith, and also a toft in Crossom, which was not mentioned in the confirmation charter. These confirmations indicate that Picot was her under-tenant in West Cottingwith.

The inheritance of Roger son of Roger did not pass directly to Emma on his death which occurred before 1190, instead passing briefly to his brother Thomas, who was deceased in 1190, then to Thomas son of Thomas, who was dead without issue before 1196. This left Emma as the sole heir of her father, Roger son of Alured.

Emma's husband, Roger de Hay, appears to have held the inheritance of Thomas son of Thomas until he came of age, as in 1191 Thomas paid into the exchequer for entry into his father's lands, of which he was disseised by Roger [de Hay].[32]

Roger de Hay was dead in 1196,[33] and his widow Emma died around 1200. The family's lands in Yorkshire then passed to their son, Thomas de Hay.

Emma of Dilolton (Diholton)

This lady is something of a mystery. Apart from her appearing in the charter of confirmation as having granted to Thicket one oxgang of land in Wheldrake, she is not mentioned again in contemporary, earlier or later records. The placename 'Dilolton' is also a mystery. However, in the *Inspeximus* and confirmation of the charter of King John to Thicket Priory granted by King Edward I in May 1285, the name is rendered 'Diholton', but with the same problems of identification as 'Dilolton'.[34]

---

[32] PRS, vol 39, NS 1, p. 66. The Pipe Roll does not give the surname of Roger, but it could only have been Roger de Hay as the husband of Thomas's only surviving relative, his aunt, Emma de Hay

[33] PRS, vol. 45, NS 7, p. 188. Emma Hay accounted for a disseisin in this year

[34] CPR, Edw I, 1281–1292, p. 165

Richard Malbis (Mallebisse)

As mentioned previously, Geoffrey de Fitling and Hugh de Bolton married the two daughters and heiresses of Thomas Darel of Wheldrake. Thomas Darel held Wheldrake under the Percys in 1166, but under the division of William de Percy's estates in 1175 Maud de Percy, Countess of Warwick, gave her nephew, Richard Malbis, the service of Thomas Darel's heirs, his daughters Beatrice and Cecily, and the Malbis family became the lords of Wheldrake, with the Darels as their vassals.

At some point Richard Malbis granted the precinct of the castle (*castellano*) of Wheldrake to Thicket Priory, as Burton informs us that Sibilla, prioress of Thickeved, and the convent thereof, quitclaimed around 1211–1214 all their right to the precinct of the castle, with one acre of land, and four other acres, that Richard Malebisse had given them.[35]

In order to date the grant of the precinct of the castle to Thicket Priory by Richard Malbis, and the bailiwick of the castle by Thomas Darel's heirs, we must look to the Chronicle of Roger of Howden, which tells us that Richard Malbis was granted a licence to fortify a castle he was building in Queldric (Wheldrake), dated 31 March 1200, but the licence was revoked due to pressure from the garrison and sheriff of York, and the building was never completed.[36] It was this setback that probably persuaded Malbis and his vassals to divest themselves of the uncompleted castle, and donate it to Thicket Priory, probably during the latter part of 1200 or during 1201.

Walter de Percy[37]

In February 1218/19 Walter granted to Thicket a carucate of land in Sand Hutton, and in addition three oxgangs lying in Norton fields between the land of Maud of Flammavill and land held of Walter by Thomas le Large; a toft

---

[35] Burton, *Monasticon*, p. 192. Burton quotes the Chartulary of Fountains, no. 38 as his source, and names among the witnesses Henry de Redman, *tunc vice com.* Henry de Redman was high sheriff from 1211–1214

[36] Roger of Howden, vol. iv, p. 117, referencing RC, *Chartarum*, p. 42. Further details on this 'castle' at Wheldrake is available on the Gatehouse website: http://www.gatehouse-gazetteer.info/English%20sites/4649.html

[37] Walter de Percy was the son of William de Percy by his second wife Sibyl de Valognes, and half brother to the previously mentioned Maud de Percy, Countess of Warwick, and daughter of William de Percy by his first wife Alice de Clare de Tonbridge

held by Wymark; and two parts of a toft held by Godard: to hold to the prioress and her successors and her church of S. Mary of Thickeheved for ever, in frankalmoign, quit of all secular service.[38] In 1219 Walter was recorded in the Fine Rolls and Pipe Rolls as owing the king one mark for a carucate of land in Sand Hutton, held of the prioress of Thicket.[39]

William, son of Peter

According to Burton, in 12 Henry III, William son of Peter, granted to the prioress and convent of Thicket ten oxgangs of land in Cottingwith, but it is not recorded in the *Feet of Fines for Yorkshire*.[40] However, there is a fine, 15 Henry III, between Eve, the prioress of Thicket, and Agnes the daughter of Peter (and sister to William son of Peter) concerning ten oxgangs of land in Cottingwith which the prioress and her church of Tykeheved hold by the gift of William son of Peter, in frankalmoign. The prioress to receive Agnes into all benefactions and prayers henceforth.

This fine was the result of an earlier case, dated 8 June 1231, in an Assize at York, in which the prioress of Tykeved summoned Agnes daughter of Peter to warrant ten oxgangs of land in Cottingwith, for which the prioress held the charter of William son of Peter, his heir; and for default of warranty the prioress was compelled to do suit at the Wapentake and County Courts. The prioress claimed one hundred shillings damages, and produced the charter by which William son of Peter gave to the nuns of Tykeheved in frankalmoign, and warranted that he and his heirs would acquit the nuns of all secular services. Agnes came and admitted the charter and warranty, and said that she would acquit the prioress of all services, as the charter witnessed. They reached a concord and had a cyrograph, and the prioress remitted her damages.[41]

---

[38] Parker, J. (ed.), *Feet of Fines for the County of York, from 1218 to 1231*. YASRS, vol. LXII, (1921), p. 24. Burton gives William de Percy as granting the three oxgangs of land in Norton, but the fine he quotes definitely says Walter de Percy

[39] Hen. III Project, 2 Hen III, no. 265; PRS vol. 80, N42, p. 197

[40] Burton, *Monasticon*, p. 280, and note c: quoting Fin. Ebor,12 Hen III, Lig. D. no. 25. No entry for this fine in the *Feet of Fines for the County of York, 1218–1231*, Parker, J. (ed.), YASRS vol. LXII, (1921)

[41] *ibid.*, p. 135–136, quoting Assize Roll 1042, m. 3

This fine presents a problem, as in *Kirkby's Inquest* for the year 1284–5 the total holding of the prioress in Cottingwith was ten oxgangs when previously we have seen that Roger son of Roger gave four oxgangs there, as did his brother, Thomas son of Roger, and a further one oxgang by Picot, totalling nine oxgangs. It was theorised that this was not a new grant of William son of Peter, but a confirmation of the nine oxgangs gifted by Roger, Thomas and Picot at the foundation, and that the missing one oxgang was the land in Thicket that Roger son of Roger had given also at the foundation.[42] This theory is more than reasonable, as the heir of these grants, Emma Hay, passed to her descendants any outstanding obligations relating to this land, and in September 1280 her great grandson, German Hay, agreed with Joan, prioress of Thicket, that he would do the king's service arising from the messuage and 10 oxgangs she held of him in Thicket and Cottingwith.[43]

Later Grants from 1250 to the Dissolution

Godfrey de Melsa (Meaux) and Isabel de Acun

This grant is assumed. Thicket Priory is listed as holding Lepton (Leppington, in the parish of Scayingham) at the Dissolution. We know that Thicket held land in Lepington after the death of Godfrey de Melsa, but before his widow, Isabel de Acun, had died.[44] This constrains the dates to *circa* 1249x1294.[45] No grant has been found to indicate who granted Thicket Priory this land in Leppington, but in the absence of any evidence it is assumed it was the lords of Leppington, Godfrey de Melsa, or his wife Isabel de Acun, who was known to German Hay.[46]

---

[42] Carpenter, p. 683

[43] Slingsby, F.H., *Feet of Fines for the County of York, from 1272 to 1300*, Yorkshire Archaeological Society, Record Series, vol. 121, p. 45

[44] Ancient Deeds, A. 291

[45] Godfrey de Melsa was alive in 1249, but his year of death is unknown, *Family of Meaux* in YAJ 43, p. 103. The will of Godfrey's widow, Isabel de Acun, is referred to in 22 Edw. I (1294), Ancient Deeds, A. 362

[46] Ancient Deeds, A. 363

Ellerton Priory

In 1264, with the consent of German de Hay, the patron of Thickeved, an agreement was made between the prior and convent of Ellerton, and the prioress and nuns of Thicket, namely: that the prior and convent would confirm to the nuns certain lands held of German's fee in West Cottingwith and Crossum, for which the prioress and nuns would give a toft in West Cottingwith, and two selions[47] of land in Lundcroft.[48]

Thicket needed the confirmation of Ellerton Priory for the lands they held in West Cottingwith and Crossom, as in the *Nomina Villarum* of 1316 it is recorded that Ellerton Priory was the lord of those places.[49]

Rather than being a grant of land, this confirmation actually cost Thicket two pieces of property. The toft they gave was almost certainly the one given by Picot in Crossom, but how the two selions in Lundcroft came into Thicket's possession is unclear.

Fountains Abbey

It has been mentioned previously that around 1211–1214, Sybil, the prioress of Thicket, quitclaimed all the right of Thicket Priory to the precinct of the castle in Wheldrake with some land that Richard Malbis had given them. But in 1290, Robert the abbot and convent of Fountains and the convent thereof, gave to Joan, prioress of Thicheved, and the convent thereof, and their successors, five acres of land next to Thickevedrave, near the land of the said prioress.[50] It is unclear if this was the same five acres that Sybil had quitclaimed.

In the Memorandum Book of Fountains, it was noted that in the period 1446–1458 Thicket paid seven pence for one acre of land in Thikheued Rayn

---

[47] A selion was a strip of land one furlong long (220 yards) by one chain wide (22 yards). Two selions equalled one acre

[48] The only place of this name I have found is near Burton Hall. Lundcroft and Burton Hall were in the township of Gateforth in the parish of Brayton. See YAJ, vol. 17, pp. 97–98

[49] Kirkby's Inquest, p. 319

[50] Burton, *Monasticon*, p. 280, and note *n*, which references page 192, and note *d* on that page, which references the Cartulary of Fountains, entry no. 39

per annum, and the same for one acre of land in Moscrofte.[51]

Thickevedrave is sometimes referred to as Thickeved Rayn. This place is not precisely identified, but is almost certainly in the vicinity of Thickhead or a part of it, possibly the drain connecting Alemare to the Derwent.

Roger de Lascelles

By an escheat in the 18th of Edw I, [20 November 1289–19 November 1290], it appears that Roger de Lascelles held land in Escrick at that time of the prioress of Thicket.[52] An *inquisition ad quod damnum* was held to determine if an alienation of this land would damage the king, which returned in the negative,[53] and consequently Roger was granted a licence, 8 April 1291, to alienate in mortmain five score acres of land in Escrick to the prioress and nuns of Thickeheved.[54]

Although not mentioned in the inquisition or licence, Joan, the prioress of Thicket, was also granted a free tenement in Escrick by Roger, and in 1300 she raised a case in the Court of Common Pleas against the heirs of Roger to exonerate her of the service which the Abbat of St. Mary's, York required for the free tenement she held of them in Escrick.[55]

William le Gra

William le Gra of York sold by Fine a messuage and 1000 acres of marsh at Sand Hutton (*pro mess. Et M. acris marisci in Sand-Hoton juxta Stainford Bridge*) to Joan, Prioress of Thikheued. William remitted and quitclaimed in court for himself and his heirs to the Prioress, her successors and her church and will warrant. For £20 sterling, by the king's command. Dated: 32 Edw I.[56]

---

[51] Memorials, *Fountains*, pp. 183, 190, 248. Moscrofte could be Molescroft (sometimes spelt as Moscrofte), a village and a township in Beverley, St John's Parish

[52] Caley J. and Bayley J., (eds.), *Calendarium Inquisitionum Post Mortem Sive Escaetarum*, vol. 1. (1216–1327), p. 103, (no. 83a)

[53] The *Inquisition ad quod damnum* for this alienation is listed in *Calendarium Genealogicum*, (Henry III and Edward I), vol. 1, p. 420 (no. 83a)

[54] CPR, Edw I, 1272–1307, p. 427

[55] TNA, Ref: De Banco, Mich. 28 & 29 Edw I, m. 259d

[56] TNA, Ref: C260/161 no. 41; *Feet of Fines for the County of York, from 1300 to 1314*, YASRS 127, p. 51

Thomas de Alwathorpe (Alwarthorp, Alverthorp)

On the 5 November 1318, at York, the prioress and nuns of Thykeheved were granted a licence to acquire in mortmain lands, tenements and rents to the value of 10 marks a year.[57] The prioress at this time was Alice de Alverthorpe, and the application for a licence was normally the first step in a pre-agreed grant by a benefactor. In 12 Edw. I (08 Jul 1318–07 Jul 1319) Thomas de Alwathorpe, applied for a licence to alienate in mortmain a house, land and rent in York, West Cottingwith and Green Hammerton.[58] Accordingly an *inquisition ad quod damnum* was conducted to determine if this would be prejudicial to the crown, or anyone else, and being in the negative a licence was duly granted, which read:

> Licence for the alienation in mortmain to the prioress and nuns of Thikeheved (or Tykeheved) by Thomas de Alwarthorpe of York of a messuage, an oxgang of land, and 15s. 1d. of rent in York, West Cottyngwith and Grenhamerton, which are held of the prioress and are worth in all their issues according to their true value 20s. as appears by an inquisition made by the sheriff of York, in part satisfaction of a licence granted to them to acquire in mortmain lands, tenements and rents to the value of 10 marks a year.[59]

This was not the first gift to a religious house that Thomas de Alwathorpe had made. In 1311 he had granted 5 marks of rent in York to a chaplain to celebrate divine service in the Church of All Saints, Ousegate, York, for the souls of Roger Haget and Ellen his wife, and of the grantor and Isabella his sister, and of their ancestors.

But who was Thomas de Alwathorpe? In 1307 he was appointed to the custody of the smaller piece of the seal for the recognizances of debts for the City of York. In 1311 he was M.P. for York, and from 1315 he was the clerk

---

[57] CPR, Edw I, 1317–1321, p. 225. For the term 'in mortmain', I would refer the reader to the relevant Wikipedia page: https://en.wikipedia.org/wiki/Mortmain

[58] A 'licence to alienate' was simply a licence to transfer ownership of property rights to another person. Nowadays this would be referred to as a freehold conveyance

[59] TNA, Ref: C 143/137/24 (*Inquisitions Ad Quod Damnum*); for the grant of the licence see CPR, Edw II, 1317–1321, p. 320

of John Malbis, late Sheriff of York, and engaged on the king's service collecting fees and dues to the crown from the county, and was bailiff of the City of York in 1316 and 1317.

Thomas's sister, Isabella, has already been mentioned, but it remains to be seen what relation Thomas was to the prioress of Thicket, Alice de Alverthorp, but they were most like close kin, if not another sister of Thomas. Alice de Alverthorpe resigned (probably due to old age) in 1335, after serving as prioress from 1309.

Robert de Lyndesey

Robert de Lyndesey of York confirmed a donation of 10s. annual rent from a tenement in Colbergate, York, to the nuns of Thikheved which [mutilated] ... de Feryby and Juliana his wife and mother of the said Robert had granted to them for fourteen years. Dated at York, the Saturday after the feast of St. Nicholas, 8 Edw III (10 December 1334).[60]

Robert de Youlton or de Yolton

At the inquisition of Robert de Yolton held in York 23 September 1350, it was found that he had the service of a bovate of land in Yolton, held time out of mind by the prioress of Thikheved in frankalmoign.[61]

Sir Robert Aske

In 1522 Sir Robert de Aske, knight, granted a yearly rent of 7s. 4d. for an annual obit 'for the souls of Robert de Aske, one of the late patrons of this house, and Elizabeth his wife'.

---

[60]Turner, p. 634
[61] CIPM, vol. 9, 1347–1352, no. 542

Foundation and Early Grants

Place	Donor(s)	Grant	Year
Thickhead	Roger Fitz Roger	Territory of. Later defined (post-clearing) as 10 oxgangs	Before 1204
W. Cottingwith	Roger Fitz Roger	4 oxgangs	Before 1204
Goodmanham	Roger Fitz Roger	1 oxgang	Before 1204
W. Cottingwith	Thomas Fitz Roger	½ carucate	Before 1204
W. Cottingwith	Picot	1 oxgang	Before 1204
W. Cottingwith	Geoffrey de Ficelingham Hugh de Bolton	Essart of land of the king's waste	Before 1204
W. Cottingwith	William, son of Peter	10 oxgangs	Before 1231
Goodmanham	Emma, sister of Roger Fitz Roger	1 oxgang	Before 1204
Wheldrake	Geoffrey de Ficelingham Hugh de Bolton	2 oxgangs each	Before 1204
Wheldrake	Emma de Ditholton	1 oxgang	Before 1204
Crossum	Picot	1 oxgang	Before 1200
Wheldrake	Hugh de Bolton with his daughter, Isolda	His part of the castle of Wheldrake, with 2 acres and a toft	1189x1199
Wheldrake	Richard Mallebisse	The castle of Wheldrake, with 5 acres	Before 1214
Sand Hutton	Walter de Percy	1 carucate	Before 1219
Norton	William de Percy	3 oxgangs	Before 1219

Notes: All of the above endowments were probably granted around the same time, during or shortly after the foundation, which was as early as Richard I (1189x1199) or even earlier, temp. Henry II, if Picot is identical with Picot de Lascelles (d. 1179), the father of Roger de Lascelles, the father of Roger de Lascelles.

I suspect Thicket was founded by Roger son of Roger, shortly after the death of his father, Roger son of Alured, who was dead by 1162.

Later Grants

Place	Donor(s)	Grant	Year
West Cottingwith and Crossum	Prior and Convent of Ellerton	Confirmation of the lands held by Thicket Priory. Thicket yields one toft in West Cottingwith, and two selions of land in Lundcroft	1264
York	Unknown	Rent-charge of 4s. 6d. per annum upon lands in York	*c.* 1279
Thikehed	Abbot and Convent of Fountains	5 acres of land at Thicket	1290
Escrick	Roger de Lascelles	5 score acres of land in Escrick	*c.* 1291
York and Sand Hutton	William la Gra of York	Lands in York, and a very large tract of land in the marsh at Sand Hutton	1304
Benetland	Unknown	Thicket Priory held this Lordship in *Kirkby's Inquest*	*c.* 1315/16
York, West Cottingwith and Greenhamerton	Thomas de Alwathorpe of York	A messuage, a bovate of land, and 15s. 1d. of rent in York, West Cottyngwith and Grenhamerton	*c.* 1318/19
York	Robert de Lyndesey of York	10s. annual rent from a tenement in Colbergate, York	1334
Yolton	Robert de Yolton	One oxgang	Before 1350
Obit	Sir Robert de Aske	A yearly rent of 7s. 4d. for an annual obit for Robert de Aske, one of the late patrons of this house, and Eliz. his wife	1522

Other Property Interests

Apart from property that was granted to the Priory, Thicket had at least one other property interest. After 1454 Thicket Priory leased Talkan Tower in York,[62] one of the city's posterns on the River Foss which was later replaced with the Fishergate Postern Tower.[63] It is not known to what purpose this lease was applied. It may have been rooms for the prioress when she was in York on business, or an office for the priory's receiver in York.

Testamentary Bequests

The numbers of bequests to Thicket are few in number, given the small size of the priory, and the sparsely populated location.

1398: Sir Thomas Ughtred bequeathed in his will to the nuns of Thicket, 40s. to pray for the souls of himself, his wife Katherine and William his son.

1402: Sir John Depeden bequeathed in his will to the holy nuns of Thicket, 20s. to pray for the souls of himself and his wife Elizabeth.

1404: Walter Berghe bequeathed in his will to the priory and convent of Thicket, 20s.

1494/5: Sir Brian Roucliffe of Cowthorpe, one of the Barons of the Exchequer, bequeathed in his will to the priory and convent of Thicket, half a mark.

1500: Edmund Thwaites of Lund, Esq., bequeathed in his will to the prioress of Thicket, 20s.

1530: Edward Saltmarshe of West Cottingwith, bequeathed in his will to the prioress of Thicket and her sisters, 3s.

---

[62] York City Archives: Bridgemasters' Rolls, C86.1, 2

[63] York was surrounded by the city walls, with several main gates through the walls, called 'bars'. Where the walls touched the rivers Ouse and Foss another four gates, called 'posterns', penetrated the walls, for pedestrians only. The posterns, all of tower construction, were manned by watchmen, but spare rooms inside a tower were occasionally leased out

Testamentary Burials

It is clear that Thicket Priory had a burial ground, or burial facilities within their chapel. The evidence for this comes in the last wills and testaments of Yorkshire testators wishing to be buried at the priory. Unfortunately, none give the precise location (e.g. in the burial ground, or in the quire [choir] of the chapel).

The following testamentary burials were extracted from the entries in the indices to *Wills in the York Registry, 1389–1553*.[64]

1405: Henry Undirwynd, to be buried in Thykhed Abbey (*sic*), vol. 3, fol. 242

1438: William Gibson of Queldryk [Wheldrake], to be buried in Thikhede Monastery (*sic*), vol. 3, fol. 540

1438: John Langton, chaplain, to be buried in the Convent of Thikhede, vol. 3, fol. 593

1491: John Beltonson of Cottingwith, chaplain, to be buried in Thikehede Priory, vol. 5, fol. 405

---

[64] *Index of Wills in the York Registry, 1389–1514*, YASRS 6, (1889); and *Index of Wills in the York Registry, 1514–1553*, YASRS 11, (1891)

CHAPTER 3

The Construction of the Priory
Building Materials – Rooms and Dimensions – Outbuildings

The size and construction methods of the original buildings that comprised Thicket Priory at its foundation in the late twelfth century are not known with certainty, but it is likely that the priory consisted of a modest wooden main building, with thatched roof, capable of accommodating the minimum number of nuns for a priory, i.e. twelve, and some outbuildings dedicated to livestock and agriculture.

The priory was also granted murage 13 Edward I, but it is not clear if this was for a containing wall around the priory or for flood defences.[65] Over the next 300 years we know the building was improved and expanded, with the addition of an upper floor, the replacement of thatched roofs with tiles and lead, the introduction of glass windows to replace shuttered windows, and the construction of further outbuildings. It is clear that the internal partition walls maintained their original construction given the ready nearby supply of withies, mud and straw.

Fortunately, we have a very detailed description of Thicket Priory taken from the Surveys conducted by the Visitors sent out by Henry VIII prior to the Dissolution of the Monasteries, which clearly shows these improvements, and gives the description of every room on both floors of the priory, plus the outbuildings, with some rooms having construction details.[66]

Thicket Priory was described thus by the Visitors:

> The church, 60 feet long by internally 18 foot broad, with a low roof covered with lead, with 5 glass windows containing 44 feet of glass, with 16 stalls in the quire, and the high altar, 2 in the quire and 1 underneath.
> Item: The cloister, at the north end of the church, 60 feet

---

[65] *Calendarium Rotulorum Patentium in Turri Londinensi* (1802), p. 52b. Murage was a toll for the repair or constructions of walls, usually around towns and cities, but also for defensive sea or river walls

[66] TNA, Ref: SP 5/2 fols. 62–63

square by 6 feet broad, covered with tiles over 1 part and 3 parts under chambers.

Item: The chapter house, at the east side of the cloister, 12 feet long by 8 feet broad, with a little glass window, 4 feet of glass.

Item: Two other low chambers by the same.

Item: The dorter [67] over the cloister and chapter and chambers, 60 feet long by 15 feet broad, covered with tiles.

Item: The brewing house and bulting house,[68] all the length of the north side of the cloister, and 10 feet broad.

Item: An old bakehouse by the same, 20 feet square, daubed walls all covered with thak.[69]

Item: The garner[70] over the brewhouse and the cloister, 51 feet long by 18 feet broad, with timber walls covered with tiles.

Item: A new wood house at the west side of the cloister, 32 feet long by 6 feet broad, and timber walls.

Item: A chamber over the same, 32 feet long by 12 feet broad, timber walls, covered with tiles, and the floor but half boarded for it is not yet finished.

Item: The new parler[71] at the west side by the church door, 24 feet long by 20 feet broad, with one bay window glassed containing 30 feet of glass and 3 other little glass windows, and timber walls with a chimney.

Item: A little buttery by the same.

Item: A new chamber over the parler, 24 feet long by 20 feet broad, with a chimney, timber walls covered with tiles and a glass window containing 12 feet of glass.

Item: A little chamber by the same over the buttery and

---

[67] Dormitory

[68] The Bulting House was the large room where meal was sifted

[69] Thak, from 'thack' or 'thatch' and similar to wattle. The daub used was straw-reinforced mud bricks

[70] The Garner was where corn was stored

[71] From the French 'to speak': a place where the rule of silence was relaxed and where business could be conducted; a place where merchants could buy and sell to the priory

cloister.

Item: A little cheesehouse between the parler and the kitchen.

Item: The new kitchen 18 feet long by 12 feet broad with a fair chimney, timber walls, covered with tiles.

Item: A chamber over the kitchen called the kitchen chamber or cheese chamber, 18 feet long by 12 feet broad, plastered floor, good timber walls, covered with tiles and no glass.

Item: A little chamber by the same, 10 feet square covered with tiles.

Item: A chamber at the nether end of the church, 14 feet square, with a chimney, a little glass window, timbered walls, covered with tiles.

A little chamber by the same, 10 feet square covered with tiles.

Item: The milk house, 8 feet square, by the kitchen.

Item: A little larder, 10 feet long and 6 feet broad.

Item: The low hall, 20 feet long by 14 feet broad with a fair chimney, a glass window somewhat broken, timber walls, covered with tiles.

Item: A little buttery at the upper end of the same by the parler, 12 feet long by 8 feet broad.

Item: The parler at the upper end of the hall, 16 feet square, with a chimney, a bay window glassed, 10 feet of glass, and timber walls and sealed above with wainscot.

Item: A chamber over the parler, 20 feet long by 17 feet broad, with a chimney, a glass window, timber walls, covered with tiles.

Item: Another buttery, 12 feet long by 10 feet broad, with a little chamber or house by the same.

Item: Another chamber over the buttery, 16 feet square, with a little glass window of 6 feet of glass, timber walls, covered with tiles.

Item: A dovecot before the hall door, 12 feet square, timber walls, decayed, ill covered with slates.

Item: A guest stable, 22 feet long by 12 feet broad, timber walls, covered with tiles.

Item: An old hay barn, 60 foot long by 20 feet broad, ill daubed walls, decayed, and ill covered with thak.

Item: A corn barn, 24/4 feet long by 20 feet broad, timber walls covered with thak.

Item: An old stable for workhorses, 20 feet long, and 14 feet broad, old daubed walls, covered with thak.

Item: An ox-house and cow-house together 24/16 feet long by 16 feet broad, daubed walls, covered with flak.

Item: The priest's chamber, 12 feet square, daubed walls covered with thak.

Item: The kiln house, 24 feet long by 14 feet broad, daubed walls, covered with thak.

Item: An old swinecot.

The references to *the new bakehouse, the new wood house, the new parler* and *the new chamber*, while still retaining the old rooms of the same names, all clearly show expansion.

The floor plans of Thicket Priory below, derived from the descriptions in the Visitor's Survey, are scaled and are largely accurate, but doorways, staircases and corridors are not mentioned in the Survey, neither are the placement of the outbuildings, so their placement has been estimated from contemporary surviving priories in England and Europe.

It is known that the priory had a mill, and is mentioned in the Survey. It was not within the priory precincts, but was probably close by. In 1683 and 1703 there were fields in West Cottingwith named Mill Hill, and Mill Hill Lands, and in 1757 a Mill Field is mentioned, which all may give clues to the site of the mill.[72] Unfortunately the tithes of Thorganby and West Cottingwith were extinguished by an Enclosure Act in 1810, so the invaluable tithe maps of the 1830s, with their listing of all the fieldnames, were not created.

---

[72] Hull History Centre: DDJ/14/112; DDJ/14/22; DDJ/14/160

Ground Floor Plan of Thicket Priory

The walls of the upper floor plan are shown in black, while ground floor rooms that are single storey are shown in dark grey, to indicate how the ground floor and upper floor are aligned.

Upper Floor Plan of Thicket Priory

Looking at the layout of the upper floor, one could imagine that the New Chamber over the Parler, and the two chambers off it, likely formed the rooms of the prioress, who was usually a lady of high birth. The nuns would have lived a dormitory life in the Dorter, and guests and the holders of corrodies would occupy the remaining chambers.

CHAPTER 4

The Economy of the Priory
Agriculture – The River and Fisheries – Corrodies – School

Some of the land granted to Thicket Priory during its foundation and later was heavily wooded, but with mostly low quality trees. This land would have to be assarted (deforested) to turn it into arable agricultural land that could be ploughed or turned to pasture. Some of the donors to Thicket mentioned that they had royal licences to deforest land they had donated, but still much needed to be done, and the nuns set about having their lands deforested, some by labourers for their demesne land, and some by potential tenants who would clear the land then lease it from the priory.

Much of the land between the Ouse and Derwent needed deforesting to make it productive, often without a direct licence by the king, but in 1234 King Henry III imposed a blanket fine on the whole of the Ouse and Derwent area for deforestation, but in quiet and full satisfaction. The fine was set at eight hundred marks, and the portion allocated to Thicket was a modest six marks and four shillings.[73] Later, on a petition from the queen, Thicket was pardoned three marks of the total sum.[74]

In Chapter 3, The Construction of the Priory, the names of the various rooms give us an insight of the sort of work the nuns were engaged in, and it is immediately apparent that the nuns were involved in modest agriculture. They did not farm all their land themselves of course, just enough for their own needs, and the rest was farmed by tenants.

Of particular importance was grain, which they stored in the Corn Barn, before threshing, with the resulting grain being stored in the Garner. After the grain was ground in their windmill the flour would be sifted in the Bulting House, and then used in the Bakehouse for their bread, and in the Kiln for drying before malting, then on to the Brewing House for the brewing of light ale for their own consumption and that of their servants, and possibly for local sale.[75]

---

[73] CCR, Hen III, 1231–1234, p. 523

[74] CCR, Hen III, 1234–1237, p. 317

[75] The difference between ale and beer was that ale did not use hops during the fermentation process, whereas beer did. The brewing of ale was a common feature of monasteries and

They also had a modest amount of livestock. The oxen would have been used for ploughing, and their cows used for milk which was stored in the Milk House, before skimming and churning to make cheese which they stored in the Cheesehouse. During the winter the oxen would be kept in the Ox and Cow Houses. The nuns also kept pigs, penned in their Swinecot; and pigeons in their Dovecot, used for their eggs and meat, and their guano for fertiliser and tanning hides; and sheep, mainly for their wool, which they would use locally, with the excess being exported.

Thicket's cattle would have been grazed on pasture, mostly consisting of meadows alongside the river, which was termed locally as Ings. In the early summer the grass would be cut for hay, which was stored for the winter period in the Hay Barn. Of course, having a navigable river on your doorstep has its advantages in terms of fish, fisheries and transport, but there were disadvantages. The low-lying area of Wheldrake and Thorganby parishes that bordered the river were prone to seasonal flooding, which if managed carefully could be turned into an advantage, as the river brought nutrients with it to enrich these lands when flooding occurred. But occasionally, the flooding was so severe that great damage was done, as was the case in July 1343, when the prioress of Thicket complained that the priory and its tenants had suffered damage from floods, due to lack of repair of the banks of a sewer. An Inquisition into the complaint concluded that the bishop of Durham and the prebendary of Rikhale [Riccall] should heighten the banks at the mouth of the sewer.[76] Again, in October, 1484, Archbishop Rotherham issued a letter asking for help for the house of the nuns of Thicket, whose fields and pasturage had been inundated by floods, and who had suffered much loss by the death of their cattle.[77]

At first sight the reader may be forgiven for thinking that the nuns also made butter, which they may have done, but the rooms called the 'Little Buttery' were in fact larders, *i.e.* rooms for storing food and drink. The nuns' buttery and the butteries for guests were kept separately.

Thicket, along with several other Yorkshire nunneries, exported a modest

---

nunneries throughout Britain and Europe, *vide* Martin, Scott C., (ed.), *The SAGE Encyclopedia of Alcohol: Social, Cultural, and Historical Perspectives*, vol. 1, (2015), p. 553

[76] CIM, vol. 2, Entry 1828

[77] Reg.Rotherham, vol. i, p. 208

amount of wool to Flanders and Italy, with Arden exporting ten sacks, Swine eight sacks, and Thicket four sacks.[78] With the Derwent being a commonly used route for the wool trade between the North and East Ridings and the great port of Hull, it would have been easy for the nuns to have their sacks of wool laden at one of the staithes in Cottingwith, though weirs on the river sometimes caused difficulties. Alternatively the wool could be carried to York less than ten miles away, by the wool collectors of the larger religious houses who operated in the area, or directly by the agents of the Italian wool merchants.[79]

It is not known what route was actually taken, or if the wool of Thicket was collected from the priory itself, but the prioress of Arden, a Benedictine nunnery thirty miles north of Thicket, said this about wool from her house: 'the Italians used to send their attorneys to Arden, within the said priory, who put the said wool in sarplers and packed it and caused it to be packed at the expense of the same merchants...and to be carried to the wool-house of Byland at Thorpe, for delivery to the said merchants.' But usually delivery was made to Clifton, a suburb of York, where the wool was loaded onto boats and sent down the Ouse to Hull.[80]

With the area around Thicket being within the demesne of Fountains Abbey, and their heavy involvement in the wool trade, it is quite possible that their agents bought the wool from Thicket.

By the fifth or sixth century, Christianity had a scale of taboos on eating terrestrial 'flesh', but western Christians in particular allowed most people to substitute fish on the roughly 130 days (35%) of the year when ideology forbade them meat. This encouraged those who could afford fish to eat it weekly and seasonally.[81]

The main rivers of the East Riding of Yorkshire, the rivers Ouse, Derwent and Hull, all fed fisheries and meres to store the non-migratory species, such as bream, perch, barbel and pike, but also migrants on their seasonal runs, eel especially, and some of these fisheries were mentioned in Domesday,[82] with

---

[78] Burton, *Nunneries*, p. 14

[79] Waites, pp. 111–121

[80] *ibid.*, p. 116

[81] Hoffman, p. 23

[82] McDonnell, p. 6. Places cited—Sutton-upon-Derwent, Coldrid (Wheldrake) and Thorganby

eel being used as a standard measure of a fishery's value.[83]

Net-caught fish were placed in artificial ponds, called stews, for later consumption, and larger meres, both natural and man-made, were used to stock and breed fish.

The Derwent had several v-shaped weirs in the vicinity of Thicket, not wide enough to prevent river navigation, though there were complaints that sometimes they did. These weirs funnelled fish into a conical basket at the point of the 'v' to trap eel and other fish. The baskets or traps were made from the abundant alder or willow withies.

The nuns of Thicket had both weirs on the Derwent and access to a part of a great mere, known as Alemare or Eelmere in the loop between the old and new courses of the River Derwent, in Wheldrake parish.[84]

At Domesday Wheldrake was held of the king by William de Percy as his tenant-in-chief. When William de Percy's estates were divided between his two daughters in 1175 Wheldrake was assigned to the earl of Warwick, the husband of William's daughter, Maud de Percy. Between *c.* 1184 (when the earl of Warwick died, without issue) and *c.* 1200 Maud gave her nephew, Richard Malbis, the lordship of Wheldrake, and Thomas Darel's heirs thus became Richard's under-tenants.[85] Richard Malbis died in 1210, and before his death he donated all his lands, possessions and rights in Wheldrake to the monks of Fountains Abbey.[86]

Following their acquisition of the lordship of Wheldrake the monks set about extinguishing the rights of their under-tenants, and common rights, to the fisheries in Alemare, and despite some resistance from the more powerful under-tenants, including the Darrell and Hay families, all resistance was overcome and the monks secured sole rights to Alemare.[87] The various surrenders, quitclaims and court cases concerning Alemare give some interesting location detail. It was located in the Ings of Wheldrake, and was

---

[83] *ibid.*, p. 2

[84] Perhaps aptly named, given that eel was the most plentiful species available, *ibid.*, p. 3

[85] VCH, *East*: vol. 3, pp. 121–123. William de Percy was the founder of the powerful House of Percy, later Earls of Northumberland

[86] *ibid.*, Cartulary, *Fountains*, vol. 2, charters 59, 60, p. 818

[87] Cartulary, *Fountains*, vol. 2, charters 139 (John Haye); 141, 142 (Geoffrey Darrell and Beatrice Darrell), and several more land holders, charters 143–148

connected to the Derwent,[88] and bordered Storthwaite on the opposite bank.[89]

Included in the list of surrenders was the quitclaim by Sibilla, the prioress of Thicket, of the priory's rights in Alemare, pertaining to their original foundation grant of Thikeheued, by Roger son of Roger, in return for the Abbey's 'counsel and aid'.[90] However, the nuns of Thicket did retain their weir and fishery on the Derwent, which was mentioned again in 1332, when several powerful lords complained that the weirs around Wheldrake and Cottingwith, belonging to the monks of Fountains and the nuns of Thicket, obstructed river traffic, to their damage. Interestingly, Fountains Abbey complained about the weir of Thicket, and Thicket complained about the weirs of Fountains.[91] There is no further mention of the weir and its fishery, and it is not listed in the Dissolution documents of 1539, nor in the subsequent Letters Patent allocating the site and lands of Ellerton Priory and Thicket Priory to John Aske, in 1542, which did list explicitly the fishery in the Derwent belonging to the dissolved Ellerton Priory.[92]

Thicket Priory occasionally granted corrodies, but always subject to a licence granted by the Archbishop of York. A corrody was similar to the modern practice of paying a lump sum to live the rest of your days in a retirement home, but in one case in Thicket a corrody was granted to a chaplain (a room, food and drink, and a small stipend), in return for his services, for life.

Non-permanent paying residents, or boarders, were also taken in, but again subject to a licence, and these will be discussed in the next chapter, and some were female children taken in for education, with a view to eventual admittance into the sisterhood. More of a monastic prep-school than a school in the general sense, but some children were sent there purely for education.

.

---

[88] Possibly by a drain, which I suspect was the Thikheued Rayn [Thickhead Drain] referred to previously

[89] *ibid.*, charters 118, 149, respectively

[90] *ibid.*, charter 147

[91] Cal. Inq. Misc, vol. 1, entry no. 1312

[92] East Riding Archives: Papers of the Aske Family, DX55/10

CHAPTER 5
Internal Community
The Prioresses – Nuns – Lay Brothers – Chaplains – Servants – Boarders

The earliest known prioress of Thicket Priory, Sibilla, occurs between 1214 and 1218, and could possibly have been the first prioress, but it is more likely that another preceded her.[93]

Sibilla

This prioress, the first recorded prioress of Thicket, occurs for the first time when she quitclaimed to Fountains Abbey the precinct and bailiwick of Wheldrake Castle. A witness to this quitclaim was Henry de Redman, Sheriff of York, who held the post of Sheriff 1211–1214.[94]

The next occurrence is dated 16 February, 1218/9, when Walter de Percy, claimant, and Sybil, Prioress of Thickeheved, tenant, were involved in a Feet of Fine concerning a carucate of land in Sandhouton.[95]

A Sibilla Hay occurs in a case of *Novel Disseisin* in October 1227, as demandent (*aramiavit*) against Richard de Murers, concerning a tenement in Elvington, which borders Wheldrake.[96] As the Hay family in the person of Roger de Hay (d. 1190–96) originally came from Sussex, and only appeared in this area of Yorkshire when Roger settled in North Cave following his marriage to Emma (d. *c.* 1200), the sister of Roger son of Roger, it is very probable that Sibilla Hay was a daughter of Roger de Hay and Emma, and sister to the known son of Roger and Emma, Thomas Hay (d. 1226–7). This Sibilla Hay does not occur again in contemporary records.

---

[93] The priory was founded before 1180, but it was quite possibly founded as early as 1162 when it is known Roger son of Alured was dead. I suspect that the three children of Roger, i.e. Roger and Thomas, sons of Roger, and their sister Emma, all of whom founded or endowed Thicket, did so probably in memory of their father. Their widowed mother is never mentioned, and I have often wondered if they had their widowed mother installed as the first prioress

[94] Chartulary, *Fountains*, no. 38

[95] *Feet of Fines for the County of York 1218–1231*, YASRS 62, no. XCIII, p. 24

[96] The Deputy Keeper of the Public Records, *Patent Rolls of Henry III, 1225–1232*, (1903), p. 160. The reader may recall that a William de Murers was a witness to the foundations charters of Emma Haye and Hugh de Bolton

Given that the patrons of religious houses often had installed one of their own kin as head, it is possible that Sibilla Hay who occurs in 1227 was the Sibilla, the prioress of Thicket in 1214, but was acting in a private suit, and using her full name. It must be stressed that this is just a theory, and more evidence is needed to confirm it, one way or the other.

Eve

Only one occurrence found, 12 June 1231, when as plaintiff, and Prioress of Tikeheved, she fined with Agnes, daughter of Peter, *impedient*, concerning ten oxgangs of land in Cottingwith.

Alice

Occurs just twice in passing. She is described as the *late* Prioress in 1279,[97] and again in 1282, both during the time that Henry was Prior of Ellerton, i.e. *c.* 1250s–1260s.[98]

Joan

Joan occurs in 1279,[99] and also from the day after Michaelmas 1280, when as *querent*, she fined with German Hay to quit her of service in the county and wapentake courts, and to grant her the tenement and lands she holds of him in Thorganby and Cottingwith in free alms.[100]

In 1282, Joan, Prioress of Thycheheved had suit against the Prior of Ellerton, to permit her to have common pasture in Cottingwith which belongs to her free tenement there, and of which Henry, late Prior of Ellerton, unjustly disseised Alice, late Prioress of Thycheheved.[101]

In 1290, Robert, abbot and convent of Fountains, gave to Joan, prioress of Thicheved and the convent thereof, and their successors, five acres of land next to Thickevedrave,[102] near the land of the said prioress.[103] This mention of

---

[97] TNA, Ref: Just 1/1056, m. 41 (Yorkshire Eyre of 1279–1281, Rex Roll of Civil Pleas); Baildon's *Notes*, vol. ii, p. 44

[98] Henry was prior during the 1250s and 1260s; the earliest found so far is 1252 (*Feet of Fines for the County of York, 1246–1272*, p. 76), and the latest found so far 1269 (Baildon's *Notes*, vol. i, 53)

[99] TNA, Ref: Just 1/1056, m. 41 (Yorkshire Eyre of 1279–1281, Rex Roll of Civil Pleas)

[100] *Feet of Fines for the County of York, 1272–1300*, YASRS 121, p. 45

[101] Baildon's *Notes*, p. 44, quoting De Banco, Mich. 10 and 11 Edward I, m. 25

[102] Probably Thickhead Rayn

'near the land of the said prioress' rather than 'near the land of the said priory', suggests that Joan held land in her own right in the area.

In 1300 Joan claimed against Thomas, son of Ivo de Gra, a house, 3 tofts, 3 oxgangs of land and 5½ acres of wood in Sand Hutton by writ of entry.[104] Joan also claimed against William, another son of Ivo de Gra, the same as above.[105]

Also in 1300: Elizabeth, widow of Roger de Lascelles claimed against the Prioress of Thicheved one third of 100 acres of land in Thickeved as her dower;[106] and Joan, the Prioress of Tykeheved against John de Curewenne, Rober le Conestable and Amice his wife, Robert de Tilliol and Maud his wife, and Ralph FitzRalph and Theophania his wife, to exonerate her of the service which the Abbat of St. Mary's York requires for the free tenement in York she holds of the defendants in Escrick.[107]

Joan occurs for the last time in 1306 in a suit against William, son of Ivo de Gra, concerning seven acres of land, eight acres of meadow, and eight and a half acres of wood in Sand Hutton.[108]

Alice de Alverthorpe

Alice is one of the few prioresses in having fairly precise dates in relation to her election, and her resignation, after serving as prioress for nearly thirty years.

In the register of Archbishop Walter Greenfield, 1306–1315, is an entry dated 12 August 1309, confirming her election, and instructing the Archdeacon or his Official to install.[109]

Alice occurs again in July 1317, when she defended an action by Alice de

---

[103] Burton, *Monasticon*, p. 192

[104] TNA, Ref: De Banco, Hil. 28 Edw. I, m. 93

[105] TNA, Ref: De Banco, 28/29 Edw. I, m. 234; Hil. 29 Edw. I, m. 35

[106] TNA, Ref: De Banco, Trin. 28 Edw. I, m. 169; De Banco, Hil. 29 Edw. I, m. 115; De Banco, Trin. 29 Edw. I, m. 145. Roger de Lascelles had granted the 100 acres to Thicket in 1290. For the inquisition, see *Yorkshire Inquisitions*, YASRS 23, p. 94

[107] TNA, Ref: De Banco, Mich. 28/29 Edw. I, m. 259d

[108] Baildon's *Notes*, vol. 2, p. 45, quoting *Inq. Ad q. d.*, file 137, no. 24

[109] Reg.Greenfield, vol.III, p. 162, no. 1491

Wighton, concerning tenements in Thykheved.[110]

On the 5 November 1318, at York, the prioress and nuns of Thykeheved were granted a licence to acquire in mortmain lands, tenements and rents to the value of 10 marks a year.[111] The prioress at this time was Alice de Alverthorpe, and in 12 Edw. I (08 Jul 1318–07 Jul 1319) Thomas de Alwathorpe, applied for a licence to alienate in mortmain a house, land and rent in York, West Cottingwith and Green Hammerton.[112]

We know that Thomas had a sister, Isabella,[113] but it remains to be seen what relation Thomas was to the prioress of Thicket, Alice de Alverthorp, but they were most like close kin, if not another sister of Thomas.

The resignation of Alice de Alverthorpe was also recorded in the register of Archbishop Melton, probably due to her old age, in 1335.[114]

Elizabeth de Haye

The nuns of Thicket elected Elizabeth de Haye unanimously as their prioress after the resignation of Alice de Alverthorpe. But the Archbishop ruled the election uncanonical, and quashed the election. But, bearing in mind the unanimity of the election he then appointed Elizabeth de Haye as prioress by his own pontifical authority, and sent a mandate to John Gower, the rector of Wheldrake to install her, dated 2 May 1335. The entry in the Archbishop's register has a memorandum attached to this entry, which states that John Gower, the rector of Wheldrake, did install Elizabeth on the same day.[115]

Elizabeth next occurs in 1337, when Agnes, daughter of James de Lissyngton complained that Elizabeth, Prioress of Thickeheved and others disseised her of houses and land in Sand Hutton. The defenders said that the property was acquired by Joan, the late prioress.[116]

---

[110] CPR, Edw II, 1317–1321, p. 81

[111] CPR, Edw I, 1317–1321, p. 225

[112] Baildon's *Notes*, vol. 2, pp. 44–45

[113] See the entry for Thomas under the Later Grants section from 1250 in the chapter on the Foundation of Thicket Priory

[114] Reg.Melton, vol. II, no. 652, p. 211

[115] Reg.Melton, vol. VI, no. 654, p. 221

[116] Baildon's *Notes*, vol. 2, p. 45

Elizabeth de Haye was still at Thicket in 1345, when she is mentioned in the will of her father, Peter del Hay of Spaldington.[117]

Hawise

Little is known about this prioress. She occurs just once in contemporary records, in 1412, when she was involved in a plea of trespass against John Atkynson.[118]

Alice Darwent

Occurs in 1432 when along with one of her nuns, Agnes Systerannes and a labourer, John Hunt of Cottingwith, they were sued by John Duram for chasing with dogs twelve cows and a hundred sheep, and inciting the dogs to bite them, so that five cows and forty sheep, valued at £7, died, and others much 'deteriorated'.[119]

Interestingly, an Alice Derwent occurs in February 1405/6 when the prior of Ellerton was commissioned by the Dean and Chapter of York, the *see* being vacant at that time, to enclose her, in a house adjoining the conventual church of Thicket. It is unclear if this refers to her as being a nun, and if she was, if this is the same Alice Darwent who became prioress. She may have been enclosed as a punishment, or had chosen to become an anchoress.

Neither the surname Darwent nor Derwent occurs in any of the York Probate Registers, nor in any of the Chancery Rolls for this period.

Beatrix

Another prioress about whom very little is known, occurring just once in contemporary records, in 1479, when she is listed among the members of The Guild of Corpus Christi in the City of York.[120]

---

[117] In Peter del Hay's will, dated 1345, he left 20s. to his daughter, Elizabeth, a nun of the priory of Thikhede (*Item do lego Elizabethæ filiæ meæ moniali in prioratissâ de Thikhede xxˢ*). Reg.Zouche, fol. 319, printed in *Testamenta Eboracensia*, Part 1, (Surtees Society vol. 4), p. 12

[118] TNA, Ref: *Coram Rege* 604, Easter, 13 Hen. IV, m. 66d; *Coram Rege* 605, Trinity, 13 Hen. IV, m. 51

[119] TNA, Ref: De Banco, Mich. 11 Hen. VI, m.507a

[120] Skaife, p. 104

Maria Dawson

Occurs as a nun at Thicket in April 1474, when she requested a papal dispensation for a defect of birth (being born of an unmarried man and an unmarried woman), that she may be elected to all offices of the order, below that of Abbess,[121] and while still a nun requested a further dispensation in May 1482, for the same reason.[122] She occurs in 1497 as prioress, when she is listed among the members of The Guild of Corpus Christi in the City of York.[123]

Katherine Chapman

Previously a nun of Clementhorpe.[124] The confirmation of Katherine Chapman as prioress of Thykhede occurred on the 23 March, 1525/6.[125] The confirmation reads:

[Marginal Heading] Sentence of confirmation of the election of the Prioress of Thicket

[Main Text] In the name of God, Amen, The merits and circumstances of the business of the election of you, Lady Katherine Chapman, sister and nun of the nunnery of Saint Clement near the walls of the City of York, elected as prioress of the nunnery of Thicket, of the order of Saint Benedict, in the diocese of York, by the Sub-prioress and convent of the same nunnery of Thicket,

Having been heard, examined, considered and fully discussed by us, Brian Higdon, Doctor of Laws, Dean of the Metropolitan Church of York and Vicar General in Spiritualties of the Most Reverend Father and Lord in Christ,

---

[121] *Registers of the Apostolic Penitentiary*, Reg. 22, fol. 206r; printed in Canterbury and York, vol. 104, no. 2306

[122] *ibid.*, Reg. 31, fol. 216r; *ibid.*, no. 2444. See also BI, Reg.23 (register of Thomas Rotherham), fol. 31. The second dispensation was probably a reissue of a mislaid dispensation, as the corresponding entry in Archbishop Rotherham's register recites the 1474 dispensation, but the entry is dated 13 January 1482/3

[123] Skaife, p. 145

[124] Clark, p. 149

[125] BI, Reg 27, (Register of Thomas Wolsey, 1514–1530), fol. 82r

Thomas, by divine mercy Lord Cardinal Priest of the title of Saint Cecilia of the Holy Roman Church, Archbishop of York, and also *legate a latere* of the Apostolic See, Primate of England, and Chancellor acting in remote parts,

And because, all the proceedings done in the aforementioned matter of the election having been scrutinised and reviewed by us, it stands clear to us, and we have found, by the acts enacted, led out, alleged, propounded, proved, exhibited, produced, testified and acknowledged in the same matter, that the said election was and is evidently canonical, correctly and canonically carried out, and your person fitting and suitable,

For that reason we, Brian Higdon, the beforesaid Dean and Vicar General in Spiritualties, the name of Christ having first been invoked, pronounce, decree and declare that the same election of you, Lady Katherine Chapman, an expressly professed nun of the Order Regular of Saint Benedict, certainly a woman with goodness of habit, knowledge of letters, commendable in merit, being of lawful age and begotten from lawful matrimony, experienced and most circumspect in matters spiritual and temporal, was and is correctly and canonically carried out, and valid and canonical in law,

And by the authority of the said most reverend father we decree that the same election is to be approved and confirmed, and in these writings we do so approve and confirm it, making good defects in the same election, if such there have been, by the same gracious authority.

By these presents, moreover, we commit to you, Lady Katherine Chapman, so elected and confirmed, the care, rule and free administration of both spiritualties and temporalities of the nunnery of Thicket aforesaid, decreeing you into the real and corporal possession of the nunnery of Thicket aforesaid, and of all its rights and appurtenances, actually to be installed in the same place by the Archdeacon of Cleveland or his Official, by induction, as is the custom.

This sentence of the confirmation of the election of Lady Katherine Chapman was read in the consistory of the Metropolitan Church of York,

On Wednesday, that is to say, the 23rd day of the month of March in the year of our Lord, according to the course and computation of the English church, 1525, in the thirteenth pontifical indiction, and in the third year of our most holy father and lord in Christ, our Lord the Pope, Clement the Seventh,

By the aforenamed worshipful Master Brian Higdon, the beforesaid Dean and Vicar General in Spiritualties,

These being then and there present; Master Tristan Teshe, Notary Public, writer of the acts of the said consistory, Sir Edward Midilton, chaplain, William Tyas, learned man, and Master John Chapman, Notary Public, Registrar etc. of the said most reverend father. [End Main Text]

Katherine was mentioned again as the prioress of Thykhede during the *Valor Ecclesiasticus* of 1535, [126] and is listed in the first draft of the Suppression Papers, 15 June 1536. Katherine is also mentioned in a York Account Roll, dated between Autumn 1537 and Spring 1537/8.[127] However, when the final draft of the suppression papers was made, 27 August 1539, Katherine's name is crossed out, and the name of Agnes Beckwith was inserted as prioress instead. It can only be assumed that Katherine Chapman had either resigned or died in the intervening period.

Katherine would only have been aged 51 years in 1539, so did she resign rather than sign the Oath of Supremacy? The fact that she was replaced, not by an existing nun at Thicket, but an outsider, Agnes Beckwith, a nun of Arthington, also gives pause for thought.

Agnes Beckwith
The last prioress of Thicket, who surrendered the priory 27 August 1539. Agnes received a pension of £6 13s. 4d.[128]

Agnes went on to marry a Gilbert Parr of York, but during the Marian Reaction, when Queen Mary reintroduced Catholicism, the marriage came before the ecclesiastical authorities in York in 1555.[129] Dr. Dakyn, the Official of the Court of Audience in York heard their confession, and imposed a relatively mild penance of fasting and prayer, but also divorced them and commanded them to abstain from cohabiting at once.[130] It is not known if they complied with this order, and with Queen Mary dying in 1558 and the reintroduction of Protestantism by her half-sister, Elizabeth I, the couple would have been free to cohabit once more if they had complied.

---

[126] *Valor Ecclesiasticus*, p. 94

[127] YAJ, vol. 42, p. 53. *Item pro bobo* [mistranscription of *pro bono*], *statu Katherine Chapman Priorisse de Thykhed, iiis. iiiid*

[128] TNA, Ref: Augmentation Books, vol. 234, p. 268b; L. & P. Hen. VIII, xv, p. 551

[129] By this time Agnes must have been around 62 years old. Dickens, p. 145

[130] BI, Chancery and Audience Act Book, 6, fol. 22v; Act Book, 7, fol. 115

Agnes was mentioned in the will of John White of York, a curate of St. Crux, St. Helen on the Walls, and St. Nicholas, and a former keeper of the Guild of Corpus Christi. In his will, dated 18 August 1572, he left a 'silver spoon' to Agnes, the former Prioress of Thicket.[131]

Agnes was still alive in 1573 but she had died by 1582.[132]

Prioresses

Period	Name	Source
Occurs between 1214 and 1219	Sybil	Burton's *Monasticon*, pp. 192, 280, quoting Chartulary de Fountains, no. 38, when Sibilla quitclaimed to Fountains the precinct and bailiwick of Wheldrake Castle. A witness was Henry de Redman, Sheriff of York, who held the post 1211–1214. Occurs in 1219, *Feet of Fines 1218–1231*, p. 24
Occurs 1231	Eve	Occurs in 1231, *Feet of Fines 1218–1231*, pp. 135–136
Before 1280	Alice	Baildon's *Notes*, p. 45. Prioress Joan, who occurs in 1280, speaks of Alice, the late prioress of Thicket
Occurs 1280–1306	Joan	Burton's, *Monasticon*, pp. 192–280; Baildon's *Notes* vol. 1, (YASRS 17), pp. 208–9. *Feet of Fines for the County of York, from 1272 to 1300*, p.45
1309–1335	Alice de Alverthorpe	Burton's *Monasticon*, p. 281, quoting Reg. William Grenfeld, p. 116, dated 2 Ides (12) of August, 1309. *The Register of William Melton*, vol. 6, no. 652 (p. 211). Memorandum that on 20 April 1335, a letter was sent to the subprioress and convent of Thicket to elect a prioress, vacant by the cession of Alice de Alverthorpe
1335–	Elizabeth de Haye	Reg. Melton, vol. 6, no. 654 (p. 211). Mandate to rector of Wheldrake to install Elizabeth del Haye, 2 May 1335
Occurs 1412	Hawise	Baildon's *Notes*
Occurs 1432	Alice Darwent	Baildon's *Notes*
Occurs 1479	Beatrix	*The Register of the Guild of Corpus Christi in the City of York*, (Surtees Society, vol. 57), p. 104
Occurs 1497, possibly 1482[133]	Maria Dawson	*The Register of the Guild of Corpus Christi in the City of York*, (Surtees Society, vol. 57), p. 145
1525 –1535	Katherine Chapman	Reg. Thomas Wolsey, fol. 82. 23 March, 1525. Also occurs 1535, *Valor Ecclesiasticus*, (Rec. Com.), vol. v, p. 94. Formerly a nun of Saint Clement at York
1539 Surrender. Last prioress	Agnes Beckwith	Received £6 13s. 4d. (Augmentation Books, vol. 234, p. 268b.) L. and P. Hen. VIII, xv, p. 551

---

[131] Cross, *Nuns*, p. 483

[132] Knowles & Smith, pp. 700–701

[133] See her listing under Prioresses above for the possibility of an earlier date of 1482

The nuns of Thicket came from a variety of backgrounds and for a variety of reasons. For many young girls a nunnery could have been the only means by which they could gain an education, which may have led some of them to embrace the merits of convent life and become a postulant on completing their studies. Sad to say, some unwanted young girls became *oblates*, typically when a father had some daughters already that he needed to find dowries for, increasing his financial pressures.[134]

In the case of young women for whom marriage was a remote possibility, convent life was often the only alternative available to the family and many fathers found it cheaper to enrol their daughters into a local nunnery, and pay the equivalent of a dowry on entry as a novice. Of course, not all girls went willingly.

For many women the religious life was a genuine calling and the Cult of the Virgin was particularly popular in the medieval period.[135] Entry into a nunnery was also a popular choice for widows. A novice might also be an older lady looking to settle down to a contemplative and secure retirement or wanting to enrol simply to prepare themselves for the next life before time ran out.

The nuns of Thicket lived under the Rule of St. Benedict, but central to the Rule were three basic vows: Obedience, Stability (staying in the house where profession was made) and Conversion of Manners (poverty and chastity).

This kind of life meant that they rarely, if ever, came to the attention of the lay authorities, and consequently very little is known about them. Occasionally they may act as a witness when the prioress defends the priory's rights in a lay court, or when they incur the disapprobation of the ecclesiastical authorities, and occasionally when they rise from the ranks of the sisterhood to be elected as the head of the priory. However, a few nuns of Thicket have been identified:

---

[134] An 'oblate' was a girl given in childhood to a convent or nunnery by her parents, to be brought up as a nun

[135] The twelfth and thirteenth centuries saw an extraordinary growth of the Cult of the Virgin in Western Europe, inspired in part by the writings of theologians such as Bernard of Clairvaux (1090–1153). *Vide* The Met Museum Essays, online at: https://www.metmuseum.org/toah/hd/virg/hd_virg.htm

Lady Elizabeth de Lasceles

Presumably, given that she is described as 'Lady', this was the widow of Roger de Lascelles, lord of Escrick, who died c. 1300.[136] Elizabeth died 1323.

Alice Darel of Wheldrake

On 5 February 1302–3 the archbishop wrote to the prioress and convent respecting Alice Darel, of Wheldrake, an apostate nun of their house, directing that if she returned to them in a contrite spirit they were to impose upon her the penance provided by their rule, but if she did not willingly undergo it, then they were to place her in some secure chamber, under safe custody.[137]

The lordship of Wheldrake belonged to Fountains Abbey at this time, and the Darels were their under-tenants. Alice was apparently an unwilling nun, so was probably a daughter of the under-tenant of Fountains in Wheldrake, but it is unclear which Darel this was.[138] She was possibly the daughter of William Darel, who held 1 carucate in Wheldrake under Henry de Percy.[139]

Margaret de Langtoft

Margaret was previously a nun in Rosedale Priory, but due to the ravages of the Scots was moved to Thicket in 1332 for protection.[140]

Agnes de Harington

Sent from Nunkeeling to Thicket for penance for her 'rebellion and obstinacy'.

Alice, daughter of Richard Griffoun

Richard Griffoun was a witness in a Proof of Age, for William Gramary, in 1355/6. At the time he said he was 70 years of age, but he remembers in the week that William Gramary was born (November/December 1333),[141] he had

---

[136] EYC, vol. v, pp. 183–186

[137] VCH, *East*, p. 124

[138] Feudal Aids, pp. 33, 173, 222

[139] CIPM, vol. v, p. 319

[140] BI, Reg. 9, (Register of William Melton), fol. 240

[141] He was born 30 November 7 Edw. III (1333)

a daughter named Alice who was made a nun in the Priory of Thikheved. So Alice's father was about 48 years old when his daughter, Alice, became a nun in 1333.

Joan de Crackenholme

On 26 January 1343–4 Archbishop Zouch wrote to the prioress and convent concerning Joan de Crakenholme, their sister nun, who was coming to them absolved from her crimes of apostasy in frequently leaving the house, laying aside her habit, as well as other excesses which are not stated. For her notorious sins the archbishop had imposed the following, in addition to her private penance. She was not to wear the black veil, or speak to any secular person of either sex, or with her sister nuns, except by leave of the prioress. She was not to go out of the cloister into the church, but was to be confined in a secure place near the church, in such a way, however, that she could be at matins and masses celebrated in the church, she was to do such things as were burdensome and not of honour, attending nevertheless divine service. She was not to dispatch any letter, or receive any sent to her. Each Wednesday and Friday she was to have bread, vegetables and light ale, and was to eat and drink on the bare ground, and on each of those days was to receive a discipline from the prioress and each of the nuns in chapter. She was to take the last place in quire, and not to enter the chapter except to receive her discipline, and was to retire immediately she had received it. Two nuns were to be appointed by the prioress as her guardians, to see to the execution of the archbishop's orders, and the prioress was to have all carried out as a terror to others.

It is one of the most severe punishments visited on any monk or nun recorded in York Registers.[142]

Isabella de Lyndesay

In April 1352 Archbishop Zouche had to write to Thicket Priory again concerning a recalcitrant nun, this time Isabella de Lyndesay, and he enjoined the Prioress to punish her after her faults were uncovered during

---

[142] BI, Reg. 10 (Register of William Zouch), fol. 154b. Printed in English in VCH, *East*, p. 124

a recent visitation of the priory by the Archbishop's commissaries.[143] The letter (translated to English) read:

William etc, to his beloved daughter the Prioress of the nunnery of Thicket in our diocese, greeting, grace and blessing.

Notwithstanding that lately, in the visitation which we made in your said house through our trustworthy commissaries, they had fittingly, lawfully and well-foundedly caused certain acts to be pursued against Isabel de Lyndesey, a fellow nun of your same house, which, in order that we might spare your reputation, we have not thought fit to be inserted into these presents,

For which acts indeed, committed by the said Isabel in peril of her soul and contrary to the decency of her order, and confessed before our said commissaries, a certain penance had been imposed and enjoined upon the same Isabel, just as seemed expedient for the health of her soul, and it had been agreed upon by instituted canons,

The aforesaid Isabel, however, taking no notice of her oath of obedience, as we take it, refusing now to enter upon the penance thus imposed upon her, led by a spirit of rebellion, does not care nor wish to undergo the discipline of her order, which she is expressly professed to follow, in peril of her soul and to the manifest scandal of the said order, and setting a very bad example to others,

Therefore we, who by virtue of the office duly committed to us are bound to call back straying sheep at the outset, like those of a good shepherd, lest the life-blood of those straying, being out of our hands, has to be looked after by a multitude in the end,

Order you, by virtue of your oath of obedience, firmly enjoining you, more strictly to compel the aforenamed Isabel to undergo and perform the corporal penance imposed upon her, and due according to the rule of your order, and accustomed to be made in similar cases.

You should not neglect certifying to us, before the coming feast

---

[143] *ibid.*, fol. 173. See more on this nun in the Archbishops' Visitations section of the External Community Chapter

of Pentecost, how the said Isabel has conducted herself in this, her penance to be performed, and whether signs of true contrition have appeared in her, since, according to her contrition, or that being absent, her resistance, this penance is worth moderating, or even increasing.

Goodbye. Given at Cawood on the twentieth day of the month of April in the one thousand three hundred and fifty second year of our Lord, and in the tenth year of our episcopacy.

Agnes Systerannes

Almost certainly the surname is not her surname at all, but the name of Sister Anne she took on becoming a nun. Agnes occurs in 1432 when along with her Prioress, Alice Darwent and a labourer, John Hunt of Cottingwith, they were sued by John Duram for chasing with dogs twelve cows and a hundred sheep, and inciting the dogs to bite them, so that five cows and forty sheep, valued at £7, died, and others much 'deteriorated'.[144]

Alice Hadilsay and Alice Broghton

Alice Hadilsay and Alice Broghton were two nuns of Thicket who gave evidence in a Cause in the Ecclesiastical Court of York in 1440/1, when the priory complained that the Prior of Ellerton was unjustly attempting to exact tithes from Thicket, while Thicket claimed to be a Cistercian house, and thus exempt. Alice Hadilsay said she had been a nun for 30 years, and was aged over 40, showing she had become a nun while still very young.[145] Alice Broghton said she had been a nun for 40 years, and was aged 49 years, again showing the very young age at which she became a nun.

---

[144] TNA, Ref: De Banco, Mich. 11 Hen. VI, m.507a
[145] BI, Cause Papers: CP F.221/1

Nuns identified to the end of the fifteenth century

Year	Name	Source
1301	Commission to the prior of Ellerton to admit the profession of Lady Elizabeth de Lasceles "*in domo de Thykheued*"	The Register of Thomas of Corbridge, Lord Archbishop of York, 1300–1304, p. 123, dated 22 Apr 1301
1303	Alice Darel of Wheldrake, an apostate	VCH Yorks. III, pp. 124
1322	Margaret de Langtoft, previously at the monastery of Rosedale, moved to Thicket for protection against Scots invaders	Reg. Melton, fol. 240
1325	Agnes de Harington, sent from Nunkeeling Priory to Thicket	Register Melton, vol. 2, nos. 384–5, pp. 114–115
1333	Alice, daughter of Richard Griffoun	CIPM, vol. 10, no. 272
1333/4	Joan de Crackenholme, said to have left her house several times	VCH Yorks. III, pp. 124
1352	Archbishop Zouch had to inflict on a nun of Thicket, for he wrote on 20 April 1352 'to the prioress, to punish Isabella de Lyndesay, a nun whose faults had been recently revealed at a visitation held by his commissaries, and the prioress was to report before Pentecost how she had behaved during the performance of her penance'	VCH Yorks. III, pp. 124
1432	Agnes Systerannes	De Banco, Mich. 11 Hen. VI, m.507a
1440/1	Dame Alice Hadilsay, aged over 40, been a nun there for 30 years	Cause Papers: CP F.221/1
1440/1	Dame Alice Broghton, aged 49, been a nun there for 40 years	Cause Papers: CP F.221/1

The next group of nuns were all those listed in the build up to the Dissolution of the Monasteries by Henry VIII following his break with Rome, and his 'Act of Supremacy', in 1534, severing the church in England from papal authority.

Following the 'Act of Supremacy', Visitors were sent to every religious house in England to survey the assets and value of each house. The resulting reports were termed the *Valor Ecclesiasticus*. This was followed by The Oath of Supremacy which the heads of all religious houses were required to acknowledge, and in 1536 Visitors were sent out again to every religious house to report on compliance, and also report on the moral character of the inmates of each house. Their reports were termed the *Compendium Compertorum*. Unlike some other nunneries in Yorkshire at this time,[146] the Visitors, Richard Layton and Thomas Lee, could find no fault with the nuns of Thicket, and all were described as '*All of good liffyng and conversacion*'.[147]

The Visitors then listed the nuns, headed by their prioress, Katherine Chapman, and was dated 13 June 28 Hen. VIII (1536). Three years later, the list was updated with a new date, 27 August 31 Hen. VIII (1539), with some ages struck out and replaced with ages three years older. Some names were struck out from the first list, showing that some nuns had either died or had left. However, some names had only one age listed, which likely indicates that the clerks doing the updating were unsure if the nuns were still there.[148]

From the following list it is clear that the prioress, Katherine Chapman, and the nun, Isabella Childe, either died or had left the house. As the list has Agnes Beckwith added to the top of the list in a later hand, it suggests that Agnes joined Thicket in the intervening period to be the prioress, rather than being elected from the existing nuns; and Margaret Swale, Isabella Cawton and Elena Fissher all appear to have joined the priory since the first list in 1536, as they are all in a later hand, or perhaps had moved to Thicket from priories that were dissolved in the first wave of dissolutions.

---

[146] For example: At Nunburmholme Isabel Thwing had borne a child, and Joan Hale had been unchaste. At Swine a priest had fathered a child upon Elizabeth Copley. Cross, p. 18
[147] TNA, Ref: SP 5/2/45
[148] *ibid.*

The list drawn up by the Visitors, and the amendments three years later

Name	Age
Agnes Beckwith (Prioress, added to the top of the list in a later hand)	46
Katherine Chapman (Prioress, struck out))	48
Isabella Childe (struck out)	60
Alice Yong	63
Margaret Kytchynman (aged 36 struck out)	39
Dorethea Knyght (aged 30 struck out)	32
Elena Sterkee	33
Matilda Chapman	27
Agnes Hunsley	27
Margaret Swale (in a later hand)	28
Isabella Cawton (in a later hand)	40
Elena Fissher (in a later hand)	26

Agnes Beckwith
Still alive in 1573, but died before 1582. See the section on Prioresses.

Alice Yong
In the list of pensioners when Thicket was surrendered in 1539, but does not appear in the next pension list of 1553 when she would have been around 77 years old. As she was awarded the second highest pension it is presumed she was the sub-prioress at that time. She certainly was the oldest.

Margaret Kytchynman
In the pension list of 1556, but missing from the list of 1564.

Dorethea Knyght
In the list of nuns during the *Compendium Compertorum* in 1536, but not in the list of pensioners when Thicket was surrendered in 1539.

Elena Sterkee (Ellen Starkey, Storkey)
Still alive and in the pension list for 1582.

Matilda Chapman
When the Visitors, Layton and Lee, came to Thicket in February 1535/6, they noted that Matilda Chapman sought release 'from the yoke of

religion'.[149] However, she was still there in 1539 when the priory was surrendered, and was recorded as still receiving her pension payments in 1582.[150]

Agnes Hunsley
In receipt of her pension up to 1564, but missing from the 1582 pension list.

Margaret (Marjorie) Swale
The only one of the pensioners in the list of 1552/3 stated to have received the monies due to her. She was still alive and in the pension list for 1582.

Isabel Cawton
Was still in receipt of her pension in 1556 and 1564, but was not in the pension list of 1582.

Elena Fisher
In receipt of her pension in 1556, but not listed in the pension list of 1564.

In addition to the nuns of Thicket there were a certain number of lay brothers in the early years of the priory. Lay brothers were those whose chose a religious life, but who did not take holy orders. They were pious and hardworking, and normally drawn from the working class, performing manual labour, or had some specific skill needed by a religious house. They would typically perform the heavy manual work, often both in the house or in the fields. Usually joining a religious house in later life, they were termed *conversi*, to distinguish them from the *oblati*.[151] Not all religious houses used lay brothers; some preferred to use hired servants.

The practice of having lay brothers in a nunnery was less than common in

---

[149] L&P, Hen III, vol. X, no. 364, p. 142. This calendar simply says '1 nun seeks release', but the actual manuscript at TNA, Ref: SP 1/102 fol. 97 states explicitly that it is Matilda Chapman who is wishing to be released, *Matilda Chapman petunt dimitti a jugo religionis*

[150] Cross, *Nuns*, p. 541

[151] Children given to a monastery or nunnery to be brought up and educated to eventually become a monk or nun

the early medieval period. It was frowned upon as time went on and eventually died out.

In the East Riding during the archiepiscopates of Greenfield and Melton, lay brothers were noticed in the Visitation Decrees of Nunkeeling, Thicket and Swine, and in Swine a Brother Thomas was nominated to be the master of the house. However, neither Nunburnholme nor Wilberfoss mention any *conversi*.

Archbishop Greenfield personally visited Thicket Priory, and followed the visitation with a decree, 1 February 1308/9, in which he decreed that no nuns, lay brothers, or inmates were to be received without his special licence.[152] Similarly, Archbishop Melton had Thicket Priory visited by commissaries in 1318/19, and his decree of 1 March 1318/9 forbad the entry of any more nuns or lay brothers, without adequate funds.

No lay brothers are ever named, and it is not known when the practice of their admittance eventually died out in Thicket, but certainly none were listed in the Suppression Papers of 1539, while servants were.

There were never any formal registration processes for chaplains at Thicket, so references to them are scant and only mentioned indirectly, in wills or the occasional corrody:

John Langtoft
In 1438, John Langton, chaplain, requested in his will that he be buried in the Convent of Thikhede.[153]

John Beltonson
In 1491, John Beltonson of Cottingwith, chaplain, requested in his will that he be buried in Thikehede Priory.[154]

Henry Wilkynson
Returned in the clerical subsidy granted in 1523, and collected in 1526/7,

---

[152] Reg.Greenfield, vol. III, no. 1219, p. 41
[153] BI, Prob. Reg. 3, fol. 593
[154] BI, Prob. Reg. 5, fol. 405

on his clear annual stipend of £4.[155] Named by the Visitors in 1536 as holding a corrody there in return for service. Henry deposed that he was above 60 years of age, and had been at Thicket for 30 years.[156]

John Holme

Also listed by the Visitors in 1536, John Holme was described as 'Chaplayne and Confessor there'.

It is remarkable that in such a small house of less than a dozen nuns in 1535, there would be a need for two chaplains. Presumably Henry Wilkynson was the chaplain for the entire priory, while John Holme was the personal chaplain and confessor for the prioress alone.

The community at Thicket typically consisted of twelve nuns, including the prioress, and being a poor priory they usually only admitted a new nun following the death of an existing nun. But add to the sisterhood the lay brothers (though no number for them is ever given), a chaplain, boarders and visitors, and the consequent necessity for the cleaning of rooms and latrines, the changing of bedding and laundry, cooking and clearing up, the care of the horses, oxen and pigs, the many agricultural tasks, harvesting, etc., the management of property and collection of rents, etc., the need for servants is obvious, even for a small house of nuns.

The evidence of servants at Thicket is scant, but they are mentioned occasionally. In 1397, the prioress of Thicket sued John, son of Henry Graunger, for forcefully rescuing his cattle which had been impounded by John Kayvill, the servant of the prioress at Benetland, for customs and services due to her.[157]

In 1432, John Duram sued the prioress of Thicket, Agnes Systerannes, her nun, and John Hunt of Cottingwith, labourer, for chasing his cows and sheep at Cottingwith.[158]

---

[155] TNA, Ref: E179/64/303, fol. 3; printed in YAJ, vol. 21, p. 249. Henry was unique in this clerical subsidy as being the only chaplain of a priory (or perhaps the personal chaplain of its prioress) listed

[156] TNA, Ref: SP 5/2 fols. 55b, 57, 58

[157] Baildon's *Notes*, vol. 2, p. 45 (Item 6)

[158] *ibid.*, (Item 8)

In the Survey of Thicket prior to its dissolution in 1539, the servants in the field book are mentioned (no names), but the nunnery servants are named explicitly and were granted rewards: Eleyn Bruce, 5s.; Mawde Bradford, 3s, 4d.; Thomas Hodgeson Cooke, 2s.; Sir John Holme Chaplayn and Confessor there, 5s.[159]

At Thicket Priory in 1309 there were five secular boarders, including Petronilla de Lincoln with her daughter of seventeen years; and three girls— Agnes de Vesey of a similar age, and two young girls, relatives of Mr John de Nassington jun.,[160] aged fourteen, and the other aged eleven. Boarders over the age of twelve years were not normally allowed, except by licence of the Archbishop, but these boarders were allowed to remain on condition that their maintenance should not burden the convent.[161] The reasons for these boarders were not given, but the three young girls were probably there to be educated, which was a common practice among the nunneries of the period. The mother and daughter is more problematic. They may have been there after paying for a corrody, if the mother was a widow, or was escaping abuse; or the daughter may have been there for education, but needed her mother's support, but this can only be speculation.

In October 1312, the prioress of Thicket was given leave by the Archbishop to receive Joan, wife of Walter de Osgodby, until Whit Sunday. Again, the reasons for this can only be speculative.[162] Three years later, in October 1315, a reason was explicit, when the prioress of Thicket was granted a licence to grant a corrody to Alice of Weighton.

As the visitation decrees to all nunneries in the East Riding in the medieval period contain a clause reminding the prioresses that is forbidden to take in boarders or inmates or to grant corrodies, without a licence, it was presumably a practice that was not uncommon.

---

[159] TNA, Ref: SP 5/2/55. Printed in Purvis, p. 88

[160] A John de Nassington was the Official (the chief judge and judicial deputy) of the Archbishop of York at this time, holding the post from 1300–1325

[161] Reg.Greenfield, vol. III, pp. xxxiv-xxxv, no. 1217, p. 39

[162] ibid., no. 1286n, p. 68

CHAPTER 6
External Community
Archbishops' Visitations – Vicegerent's Visitations – Heraldic Visitations –
Relationship with Ellerton Priory – Local People

Thicket Priory has been the subject to visitation over the course of its existence and beyond. The main visitations were those conducted by the Archbishop of York in his role as the Bishop of York, rather than in his archiepiscopal capacity; the visitations conducted by the commissioners sent by Thomas Cromwell, the vicegerent and vicar-general of Henry III, following the break with Rome; and the later visitations conducted by the heralds to inspect arms in surviving religious houses.

Archbishops' visitation decrees were usually very formulaic, and many of the same articles were sent to other nunneries following visitation and do not imply that any rules were being broken or needed correcting, but simply a reminder of what was expected.

The nuns were required to follow the rule of their order, observe silence, not leave the convent without leave, and then only to visit friends or relatives for a maximum of two weeks, and always in the company of another nun. They were to tend the sick (if they had an infirmary) according to the illness, with a nun best skilled in that illness. No nuns were to be admitted for money, and any repairs that the visitors noted were to be implemented. All nuns were to be present at service and the kitchen area was to be kept clear of seculars. Accounts were to be submitted to the archbishop's office, and the common seal of the house and all charters were to be kept under lock and key. The prioress should avail herself of the counsel of the other nuns, and no corrodies, pensions, leases or sales of land should be allowed without licence of the archbishop. The sisters and lay brothers should have differing habits, and be kept in separate quarters.

The above articles were typical, so visitation decrees need to be studied carefully to see if any articles were out of the ordinary and only those articles, in addition to the above, or with interesting qualifiers, will be noted below.

The first Archbishop of York, whose register survives, is Walter de Gray (1215–1255), and we know that during his pontificate he was conducting visitations of his diocese.[163] The Bishop of Durham was also conducting visitations around this time, and the practice extended to bishops throughout England and in France.[164]

Walter de Gray's successors as archbishop, Walter Giffard and William Wickwane also conducted visitations, but not of Thicket.[165] It wasn't until the next archbishop, John le Romeyn, that we find the first recorded mention of Thicket Priory concerning visitation, but it was only a notice of an intent to visit, but no result of the visitation is recorded, nor of it ever having happened.[166] The brief pontificate of Henry Newark (1298–1299) also has no mention of Thicket Priory, nor of his successor, Thomas Corbridge (1300–1304).

Archbishop's Visitation of 1308/9

The first visitation for which the result is known occurs during the pontificate of William Greenfield (1306–1315). There is no recording of the intention to visit, but the decree following the visitation is fully recorded, which was dated 1 February 1308/9. The visitors appointed to conduct the visitation were William de Beverley and Nicholas de Carleton, and their remit was to correct and reform. The decree did not note anything out of the ordinary.

Archbishop's Visitation of 1314/15

On the 16 January 1314/15 notice was sent to the prioress and convent of Thicket of an intended visitation, on Monday, the day after the Purification (3 February 1314/15). Following the visitation, conducted by the archbishop himself,[167] the decree was issued on the 6 February.[168]

---

[163] For example, the visitations of St. Mary's Abbey, York, and Selby Abbey. Reg.Gray, pp. 152, 327

[164] Cheney, p. xiv

[165] There is one reference to Thicket Priory in the Register of Walter Giffard, which was an instruction to his bailiff to pay the priory three shillings in alms, *Item monialibus de Thikheheved apud Cawode iiis*. By contrast, the nuns of Wilberfoss received 20s., the nuns of Nunburnholme [Brunn], 20s., and the nuns of Kirklees [Kirkeleye], 5s. Reg.Giffard, p. 123

[166] Reg.Romeyn, vol. I, no. 564, p. 203

[167] Reg.Greenfield, vol. 3, p. xxi

[168] *ibid.*, no. 1343, p. 97

No nun to leave the enclosure of the priory without the permission of the prioress or sub-prioress. The prioress to live with the convent, and take its advice on business matters. No sister to wear the black veil.[169]

These articles suggest that some nuns had left the confines of the priory without permission, and the prioress wanted to make the visitors aware of this fact and to remind the nuns that this was forbidden, and the archbishop and his visitors would be keeping an eye on things. The articles concerning the prioress living 'with' the convent and on 'business matters' suggests that complaints had been made by one or more of the nuns, that the prioress had been living outside of the priory, and that she had made some foolish business decisions. The article on not wearing the black veil is curious, as it was the normal practice in Catholic countries for novice nuns to wear a white veil and for professed nuns who had taken their solemn vows to wear a black veil.

Shortly after the decree, on the 7 March, in what looks like a separate incident, a Commission was issued to Master J. Gower, the rector of Wheldrake, to absolve the nuns, sisters and lay brothers of Thicket from the laying of violent hands upon each other, which did not draw blood (one wonders what the fracas was all about), and from admitting nuns upon payment of money.[170]

The following October of 1315 the archbishop granted a licence to the prioress and convent of Thicket to grant a corrody to Alice of Weighton.[171]

Archbishop's Visitation of 1319/20

A mandate was sent to the prioress and convent of Thicket to attend the archbishop's visitation of their house, (not at their house, but in the cathedral), dated 14 February 1319/20. However, this was superseded by a Commission issued on the 18 February to the rectors of Brandesburton and Hemsworth, to visit the nunneries of Thicket and Arthington.[172] Following the visitation in late February the decree was issued on the 1 March.[173]

---

[169] *ibid.*, no. 1350, pp. 100–102
[170] *ibid.*, p. xxxv; no. 1356, pp. 103–104
[171] *ibid.*, no. 1375, p. 110
[172] Reg.Melton, vol. 2, nos. 73 and 75, p. 36
[173] *ibid.*, no. 78, pp. 37–39

Article (10) in this visitation is noteworthy, in that it enjoined the prioress, under permitted penalties, to love and cherish her fellow nuns. Article (11) is also unusual in that it is emphasised, under penalty of removal from office and excommunication, to desist from charging for services and duties which they should provide as of right. Following the articles the visitors wrote that these were 'beneficial' warnings.

Archbishop's Visitation of 1332

A citation for the visitation of Thicket was sent out 3 April 1332,[174] and the visitation occurred on Tuesday, 29 April.[175] Unfortunately no resulting decree is recorded in the archbishop's register.

Archbishop's Visitation of 1352

Thicket was once again visited in late March 1352, and on this occasion a rebellious nun was found by the commissaries. It was serious enough (but so serious the archbishop would not put it in writing) for the archbishop to write to the prioress to inflict upon the nun a punishment, as penance. The letter reads:

> Letters to enforce [one] of the nuns to perform the penance enjoined upon her for certain acts discovered in the visitation by the commissaries
>
> William etc., to his beloved daughter the Prioress of the nunnery of Thicket in our diocese, greeting, grace and blessing.
> Notwithstanding that lately, in the visitation which we made in your said house through our trustworthy commissaries, they had fittingly, lawfully and well-foundedly caused certain acts to be pursued against Isabel de Lyndesey, a fellow nun of your same house, which, in order that we might spare your reputation, we have not thought fit to be inserted into these presents,
> For which acts indeed, committed by the said Isabel in peril

---

[174] *ibid.*, no. 385, p. 149
[175] *ibid.*, no. 484, p. 181

of her soul and contrary to the decency of her order, and confessed before our said commissaries, a certain penance had been imposed and enjoined upon the same Isabel, just as seemed expedient for the health of her soul, and it had been agreed upon by instituted canons,

The aforesaid Isabel, however, taking no notice of her oath of obedience, as we take it, refusing now to enter upon the penance thus imposed upon her, led by a spirit of rebellion, does not care nor wish to undergo the discipline of her order, which she is expressly professed to follow, in peril of her soul and to the manifest scandal of the said order, and setting a very bad example to others,

Therefore we, who by virtue of the office duly committed to us are bound to call back straying sheep at the outset, like those of a good shepherd, lest the life-blood of those straying, being out of our hands, has to be looked after by a multitude in the end,

Order you, by virtue of your oath of obedience, firmly enjoining you, more strictly to compel the aforenamed Isabel to undergo and perform the corporal penance imposed upon her, and due according to the rule of your order, and accustomed to be made in similar cases.

You should not neglect certifying to us, before the coming feast of Pentecost, how the said Isabel has conducted herself in this, her penance to be performed, and whether signs of true contrition have appeared in her, since, according to her contrition, or that being absent, her resistance, this penance is worth moderating, or even increasing.

Goodbye. Given at Cawood on the twentieth day of the month of April in the one thousand three hundred and fifty second year of our Lord, and in the tenth year of our episcopacy.[176]

Isabel's 'crimes' are not mentioned, but previously, Archbishop Zouche

---

[176] BI, Reg. 10 (Register of William Zouch), fol. 173

had written to the prioress in 1343/4 about another recalcitrant nun, Joan de Crackenholme, who had committed apostasy by frequently leaving the house, without her habit, and other 'excesses'. The archbishop lay down one of the most severe punishments ever laid down for any monk or nun recorded in the York Registers.[177]

The registers of the Archbishops of York from 1352 to the dissolution of Thicket in 1539 have not been published, with the exception of the pontificates of Robert Waldby (1397), Richard Scrope (1398–1405), and part of the register of Thomas Rotherham (1480–1500).[178] Unfortunately, none of these registers contain any visitation material for Thicket.

The two main visitations of Thicket undertaken by agents of Thomas Cromwell, the vicegerent and vicar-general of Henry VIII following the break from Rome, were the so-called *Compendium Compertorum,* and the follow-up visitation where the visitors attempted to persuade the prioress of Thicket to surrender the priory, and offering pensions if the prioress and convent agreed. Both visits were in 1536.

Vicegerent Visitations of 1536
The *Compendium Compertorum* had none of the licentious allegations against Thicket that many other religious houses had levelled against them, the only comment being that one nun, Matilda Chapman, wished to leave.[179]

When the visitors drew up their first list of the prioress and nuns of Thicket later in 1536 with the proposed pension amounts by their names, the list was headed by the brief comment 'All of Good Lyffing and Conversacion'.[180]

From the early sixteenth to the late seventeenth centuries the heralds carried out visitations, county by county, in order to regulate the use of arms, and who was allowed to bear them. Yorkshire was visited several times during this period, and occasionally churches and the remains of dissolved religious

---

[177] BI, Reg. 10 (Register of William Zouch), fol. 154b. Printed in English in VCH, *General,* p. 124
[178] Reg.Waldby; Reg.Scrope; Reg.Rotherham
[179] TNA, Ref: SP 1/102, fol. 97
[180] TNA, Ref: SP 5/2 fol. 48

houses were visited to see what arms were depicted in the stained glass windows and in memorials and brasses etc. One of the most comprehensive exercises conducted by the heralds was the visitation of 1584.

Heraldic Visitation of 1584

The visitation undertaken by Robert Glover, Somerset Herald, in 1584, is unique in all the printed visitations by the heralds in that it included all the arms noted by Glover in the houses of the gentry in Yorkshire, and in the churches and remains of dissolved religious houses.

Unfortunately, no arms were found in Thicket Priory, unlike nearby Ellerton Priory, a priory of Gilbertine monks, just across the River Derwent, which had many examples of heraldic arms in the windows of the church of the priory which had been retained as a parish church.[181] The arms were those of the benefactors of Ellerton Priory, and have survived today, largely intact, and can now be seen in the window facing the north aisle of Selby Abbey, where they were removed to in 1984 prior to the rebuilding of Ellerton Priory Church (but never returned).[182]

Ellerton Priory was founded *c.* 1207 by William, son of Peter, who was closely connected to the Hay family, the patrons of Thicket Priory,[183] who also became the patrons of Ellerton Priory.[184]

Ellerton Priory was the closest religious house to Thicket, being just two miles south of Thicket, on the other side of the River Derwent, but easily reachable via the ferry at Bubwith, which is known to have existed from at least the twelfth century,[185] and perhaps even nearer at East Cottingwith.[186]

Shortly following the foundation of Ellerton Priory, their patrons, the del Hay family, granted the church of the neighbouring parish of Aughton. The

---

[181] Foster, p. 441. Manuscript with extra detail is in the British Library, Dept. of Mss, Harl.Ms. 1394

[182] http://www.ellertonpriory.co.uk/stainedglass.htm

[183] The pedigree showing the relationship between these two families has been given by Carpenter, vol. 2, p. 678

[184] http://www.ellerton.info/history/ellerton-priory.html; VCH, *General*, vol. III, p. 252

[185] http://www.bubwith.net/history/economic-history.html

[186] http://www.aughton.info/history/economic-history.html

parish of Aughton had two chapelries, East Cottingwith, and Thorganby on the other side of the River Derwent, upon which stood Thicket Priory.[187]

Thus, through proximity, patronage and ecclesiastical ties, the two priories were closely linked. However, although the two priories were physically near each other, their status and influence were miles apart. Ellerton was well endowed and much more prosperous than Thicket, and in the eleventh and twelfth centuries monasteries vastly outnumbered nunneries, not only in England, but throughout Europe. As Burton pointed out, this state of affairs 'reflected a society in which the male element was dominant, in which endowments for religious houses were for the most part provided by men who accordingly founded monasteries for political and social reasons, as well as from a certain prejudice against women in the religious life. This was manifest not so much in a belief that women could not, or should not lead their lives in religious communities, which indeed they had done since the very early days of the Christian church, but rather in the attitude that their prayers were somehow less effective than those of men'.[188] It is somewhat telling, that by the time of the Dissolution of the Monasteries, not one nunnery in Yorkshire came above the £200 clear annual value to escape the first Dissolution Act.

The first recorded interaction between the two priories came in 1282, when Joan, the prioress of Thicket, sued Adam, the prior of Ellerton, to permit her to have common of pasture in West Cottingwith which belonged to her free tenement there, and of which Henry, the late prior of Ellerton had unjustly disseised Alice, the late prioress of Thicket.[189]

In the early 1400s more serious tensions began to arise between the two priories when the prior of Ellerton began to claim tithes from Thicket, which in 1441 led to a tuitorial appeal being filed in the Ecclesiastical Court of York.[190] Thicket was claiming that it was a Cistercian house, and therefore exempt from tithes, while Ellerton was claiming that Thicket was a Benedictine house and therefore subject to tithes. Fortunately, several of the Cause Papers concerning this case have survived, including notarial

---

[187] Reg.Scrope, vol. 1, no. 438, p. 66

[188] Burton, *Nunneries*, p. 2

[189] Baildon's, *Notes*, vol. ii, p. 44

[190] Burton, *Causes*, pp. 68–71

instruments authenticating the appeal by Thomas Fosseton, one of the proctors for Thicket,[191] who outlined the case for Thicket in the *Positions*:[192]

In the name of God, Amen, Before you, O Lord Official of the Court of York, or your Commissary General, or another competent judge, the proctor of the religious women the Prioress and Convent of the house or priory of nuns of Thicket, of the Cistercian order or the rule of Saint Benedict, in the diocese of York, in the name of his procuracy for the same, says and proposes in law, [against the religious] men the Prior and Convent of Ellerton, of the order of Saint Gilbert, in the said diocese, and against anyone at all appearing lawfully for the same before you for judgment, and against all and singular others having or who can have an interest in the matter of the underwritten appeal for protection, lawfully interposed at the said Court of York,

That it is lawful for the aforenamed ladies, the Prioress and Convent of Thicket, who had been and were of good fame, honest conversation, unimpaired opinion and full estate, and free from all reproach, to be freed of and totally immune from payment of whatsoever tithes arising from lands, places and newly tilled land, cultivated by their own labours or hands, or at their own costs, or from foodstuffs of their animals,

And to be in possession of the abovesaid immunity, and of all and singular temporalities and spiritualities annexed to the said priory of Thicket and appertaining to the same ladies in any way whatsoever, and of all tithes of their lands etc above mentioned, according to the exigency of the common law and the privileges of the Holy Roman Fathers and Pontiffs granted to them by the generosity of Kings,

And to be in possession, or rather for these fruits and foodstuffs of their animals, and of sheaves and hay cultivated and nourished at their own costs or by their own labour as is aforesaid, to be had and received, without payment of tithes of the same.

And they shall possess them canonically, and they shall effectively pursue all and singular the things set out before,

Peacefully and quietly reassuring, supporting and approving all and singular those having an interest in this regard, and especially the

---

[191] BI, Cause Papers, Ref: CP.F.221/2–3
[192] *ibid.*, CP.F.221/6

Prior and Convent of Ellerton aforesaid, saving the things to be said below.

And albeit also, on the part of the said ladies, that they are well known to be in possession or the equivalent of all and singular the premises, they are anxious about the premises, or any of them, from certain probable and credible causes gravely anticipated by them to be possible, or at least in fact for some prejudice to be created in the future,

If anyone at all, by any authority, in anyone's name or place or by their order, should unduly attempt anything contrary to the premises, or any of them, or should cause anything in any way to be attempted, it shall and may be appealed directly to the Holy Apostolic See, and come to the Court of York for protection, openly and publicly summoned and to be summoned.

Moreover, the aforenamed Prior and Convent of Ellerton, well known to be aware of all and singular the premises, and after, contrary to and notwithstanding [the appeal and summons], have unduly molested, disquieted and disturbed the aforenamed ladies being in possession of all the premises, or have ordered, caused and threatened them to be molested, disquieted and disturbed concerning the tithes of all sheaves and hay arising from lands [cultivated] by their labours and at their costs, as is aforesaid, and they do at present so order, cause and threaten them, many times and unjustly,

And they did and do inconsiderately and heedlessly impede those ladies in their possession of these fruits of their labours according to the exigency of the common law and of their abovesaid privileges and indults, [not allowing them] to enjoy, to freely dispose of the same, and to receive and be able to have the same, as they ought, and they did and do have this molestation, disquieting, threatening, impedence and disturbance done, approved and, equally, accepted, in their name, concerning misappropriating these their fruits, unduly threatening them with harm in law, and the prejudice and oppression of those ladies, heedlessly offending against sentences and censures of the said Roman Fathers the Pontiffs solemnly carried out against delinquents in this regard.

Whereupon on behalf of the said religious ladies, perceiving themselves and their aforesaid conventual house to be unduly burdened by the oppressive premises, from all and singular the same oppressions, and from each of them, and on account thereof, and of each of them, and which can be recollected by them and by each of them, there is an appeal for protection in this regard directly to the Holy Apostolic See, and it comes to the abovesaid Court of York, and it is lawful.

Which things were and are true, public, well known and manifest in the city and diocese of York, and in neighbouring places, and by the aforenamed Prior and Convent of Ellerton, and sufficiently acknowledged by their party [representing them] in the presence of the other party, from certain causes and knowledge,

And there was and is public voice and fame concerning these things.

For which reason the said proctor, in the name which is above, seeks that those things in this regard which were to be proved may be sufficiently proved in this regard for the aforesaid Prioress and Convent of Thicket, and he in their name, to be decreed to be protected, with effect, and the benefit of this protection to be granted to the same ladies and their proctor in their name according to the protective quality and nature of this matter, and the laudable customs and statutes of the said court to be observed in these premises by you, the Lord Official or your Commissary or other competent Judge abovesaid in this case,

And indeed that all and singular these oppressions, attempted after and contrary to the summons and appeal abovesaid, to the prejudice of the aforenamed ladies and their house and the party [representing them], in general, and in so far as it is possible to be clear concerning them, in particular, be revoked and duly reserved according to the laudable customs and statutes of the said court, and further for that which is just to be done for him in the premises, and in anything concerning them, according to the nature and quality of the same in all things.

The said proctor, in the name which is above, says and seeks, and intends to prove, these things, and he himself offers such things, jointly and severally, to be proved as are sufficient for it in this regard, always saving the benefit of law.

Thicket produced several witnesses to testify, by written deposition, that Ellerton had indeed been attempting to force the payment of tithes from Thicket, and depositions were brought before the court by two of the nuns of

Thicket:

> *Dame Alice Hadilsay*, aged over forty, deposed that she had been a professed nun there for 30 years, and further deposed that in autumn of the previous year she had been in the church of Thicket when the prior of Ellerton with his men had appeared in person to demand the prioress pay tithes before the removal of any hay, sheaves of corn, or any other harvest from lands within the parish of Aughton, the church of which belonged to Ellerton, and that later on the same day, she was in the hall of the prioress when two canons of Ellerton, with the authority of the church of York, forbade the removal of hay from the nunnery lands of Aughton.
>
> *Dame Margaret Broghton*, aged 49 years, and a nun for 40 years (*sic*), gave a similar deposition.[193]

Further depositions were given by local people:

> *Robert Barker*, aged 53 years, of Wheldrake, deposed that he had been born in the parish of Wheldrake, close to Thicket Priory, which had several pieces of arable land and seven acres of meadow, and throughout his lifetime had cultivated these at their own expense. He had seen their servants take away sheaves and hay, without any payment of tithe. This had been done from time out of mind and was openly believed by the people of Wheldrake. It was, he claimed, six years ago that the canons of Ellerton had first unjustly taken tithes from certain lands. He was not able to depose on the second position, but on the third he had heard tell that the prior had, the previous autumn, gone with one of his canons to the house of Thicket and had threatened the nuns. He was also unable to comment on the fourth point, but on the final article he confirmed that all the matters were indeed well known in Wheldrake.
>
> *Nicholas Darrel*, aged 67 years, of West Cottingwith; Henry ..., aged 60 years, of Thorganby (which he stated to be half a mile from the nunnery), aged sixty-seven, attested in much the same manner. However, he claimed that it was fourteen years ago when the prior and certain canons of Ellerton had taken tithes of sheaves and wheat from a certain close or lands, called vulgariter 'intake', and carried them off

---

[193] BI, Cause Papers, Ref: CP. F. 221/1

on their shoulders. He attested that the previous autumn the prior of Ellerton had gone to the conventual church of Thicket and had forbidden the nuns to remove hay, sheaves, or harvest from their lands and meadows. The witness, Nicholas, saw this as, he claims, did John Stillingfleet, William Grayve, John Lange the younger, and Robert Hueson of Cottingwith.

Henry Qweldryke of Thorganby, of the age of 60 years and more, a witness admitted, sworn, and diligently examined upon the libel annexed to these presents,

Examined and questioned upon the first particular, he says he believes this particular to contain the truth,

Because he says that he has had notice for the 40 years last past that the priory or house of nuns of Thicket, which priory of house the libel concerns, and because, as he says, for all those years he has made his home continuously in the town of Thorganby, distant by the space of half a mile, as it were, from the same conventual house, and so far as he ever knew or understood, up to the time the present dispute was moved, as he says, the prioress and convent of the aforesaid house or priory, were and are totally free and immune from all and all manner of payment of any tithe of sheaves and hay from their own lands and meadows occupied and cultivated at their own costs, or arising from foodstuffs of any of their animals whatsoever,

And moreover he says he has often heard it said that five or six years ago the Prior and Convent of Ellerton disturbed the aforesaid religious women, in possession of the premises to the extent that they carried and moved away the tenth parts of sheaves arising from certain lands of the aforesaid nuns, cultivated at their own costs in their cells, to other remote places, and disposed of the same as it pleased them,

And [they did] this unjustly as he believes just as he, having been sworn, believes, as according to the belief of this sworn man, as he says.

And otherwise, having been examined, he says he knows not how to depone upon this particular.

Examined and questioned upon upon the 2nd particular, he knows not how to depone, as he says.

Upon the 3rd and 4th particulars, he says he knows not how to depone, except from the statement from what he has heard of others.

Examined upon the 4th last particular, he says that the premises deponed by him were and are public, well-known and open matters in

the aforesaid town of Thorganby and other towns surrounding it, and
the public voice and fame in the same place laboured for a long time,
and still do labour, upon the same.

And he has not been led, instructed, bribed or incited to depone just
as he has above deponed, as he says on his oath.[194]

The cause papers also contained the appointment of the proctor for
Ellerton, and the proctors for Thicket, Robert Chigwall, William Byspham,
John Saxton and Thomas Fosseton,[195] and in addition to the depositions the
Positions document contains on the dorse, the names of the deponents, plus
three other names: *Thomas Barnebe* of Topcliffe; *Robert Hudeson* of
Thorganby; and *William Skelton* of Thorganby.

But the key document for Thicket was a Papal Bull of Pope Gregory IX,
dated at Rieti, 8 May 1228, which provided the evidence for their exemption
from tithes:[196]

Papal Bull of Pope Gregory IX
(Transcription, Latin)

*Gregorius Ep[iscopus] servus servor[um] dei dilectis in χρ[ιστ]o
filiab[us] P[ri]orisse Monast[er]ii de Thiccheheved Cist[er]ciens[is]
Ordinis eiusq[ue] Sororib[us] t[a]m p[rese]ntibus q[ua]m futur[is]
regulare[m] vita[m] p[ro]fessis In p[er]p[et]u[um] Prudentib[us]
virginib[us] que sub habitu religionis accensis lampadib[us] p[er]
op[er]a s[an]c[ti]tatis iugit[er] se p[re]parant obviam sponso ire*

*Sedes Ap[osto]lica debet patrociniu[m] impartiri ne forte
cuiusli[be]t tem[er]itatis incursus aut eas a p[ro]po[s]ito revocet aut
robur quod absit sacre religionis infringat*

*Eap[ro]pt[er] dilecte in χρ[ιστ]o filie v[est]ris iustis
postulac[i]o[n]ib[us] clement[er] a[n]nuim[us] et Monast[er]iu[m]
v[est]r[u]m de Thiccheheved in quo divino estis obsequio mancipate
sub b[ea]ti petri et n[ost]ra protecc[i]o[n]e suscipimus et p[re]sentis
sc[ri]pti p[ri]vilegio co[m]munimus*

In p[ri]mis siquid[em] statuentes ut ordo Monastic[us] qui

---

[194] Unfortunately, neither the articles (particulars or questions) that were put to the witnesses,
nor the libel, survive

[195] BI, Cause Papers, Ref: CP. F. 221/8

[196] *ibid.*, CP. F. 221/5

*s[e]c[un]d[u]m deu[m] et b[ea]ti B[e]n[e]dicti regula[m] atq[ue]
Instituc[i]o[ne]m Cist[er]cien[sium] fratru[m] in eod[em]
Mon[asterio] institut[us] esse dinoscit[ur] p[er]petuis ib[ide]m
temporib[us] i[n]violabilit[er] obs[er]vet[ur]*

*P[re]t[er]ea quascu[n]q[ue] possessiones quecu[n]q[ue] bona
id[em] Monast[er]iu[m] imp[re]senciar[um] iuste et can[oni]ce
possidet aut in futuru[m] [con]cessione pontificu[m] largicione
Regu[m] v[e]l p[ri]ncipiu[m] oblac[i]o[n]e fideliu[m] seu aliis iustis
modis p[re]stante d[omi]no pot[er]it adipisci firma vobis et hiis que
vobis successerint et illibata p[er]maneant*

*In quib[us] hec p[ro]p[ri]is duxim[us] exp[ri]menda vocabulis
locu[m] ip[su]m in quo p[re]fatu[m] Monast[er]iu[m] situ[m] est
cu[m] o[mn]ib[us] p[er]tinen[ciis] suis cu[m] pratis t[er]ris vineis
nemorib[us] ulnagiis et pascuis in bosco et plano in aquis et
molendinis in viis et semitis et o[mn]ib[us] aliis lib[er]tatib[us] et
i[m]munitatib[us] suis*

*Sane labor[um] v[est]ror[um] de possessio[n]ib[us] habitis ante
consiliu[m] gen[er]ale ac ecia[m] novaliu[m] quo p[ro]p[ri]is
ma[n]ib[us] aut su[m]ptib[us] colitis sive de ortis et virgultis et
piscac[i]o[n]ib[us] v[est]ris v[e]l de nut[ri]mentis a[n]i[m]aliu[m]
v[est]ror[um] nullus a vobis decimas exig[er]e v[e]l extorquere
p[re]sumat*

Liceat quoque vobis &c

*P[re]t[er]ea om[n]es libertates et i[m]munitates a
p[re]decessorib[us] n[ost]ris Romanis Pontificib[us] ordini v[est]ro
concessas n[ec]non et libertates et exempc[i]o[n]es secular[u]m
exacc[i]onu[m] a Regib[us] et p[ri]ncipib[us] v[e]l aliis fidelib[us]
inviolabilit[er] vobis indultas auc[torita]te ap[osto]lica
confirmam[us] et p[re]sentis sc[ri]pti p[ri]vilegio co[m]munim[us]*

*Dec[er]nim[us] ergo ut nulli o[mn]ino homi[num] liceat
p[re]fatu[m] Mon[asterium] tem[er]e p[er]t[ur]bare aut eius
possessiones auferre v[e]l ablatas retinere minuere seu quibusli[be]t
vexac[i]o[n]ib[us] fatigare*

*Sed om[n]ia integra [con]serve[n]t[ur] ear[um] p[ro] quar[um]
gubernac[i]o[n]e ac sustentac[i]o[n]e concessa sunt usib[us]
o[mn]imodis p[ro]futura Salva Sedis Ap[osto]lice auc[torita]te*

*Si qua igit[ur] in futur[um] eccl[es]iastica s[e]c[u]laris ve
p[er]sona hanc n[ost]re constituc[i]o[n]is pagina[m] sciens cont[ra]
eam tem[er]e venire te[m]ptav[er]it secundo t[er]ciove co[m]monita:*

71

nisi reatu[m] suu[m] congrua satisfacc[i]one correx[er]it potestatis
honorisq[ue] sui careat dignitate rea[m]q[ue] se divino judicio
existere de p[er]pet[ra]ta iniquitate cognoscat et a sac[ra]tissimo
corp[or]e et sang[ui]ne dei et d[omi]ni rede[m]ptoris n[ost]ri Jh[es]u
χρ[ιστ]ι aliena fiat atq[ue] in extremo examine districte s[u]biaceat
ultioni

    Cunctis aute[m] eid[em] loco sua iura s[er]vantib[us] sit pax
d[omi]ni n[ost]ri Jh[es]u χρ[ιστ]ι quatin[us] et hic fructu[m] bone
acc[i]o[n]is p[er]cipia[n]t et apud districtu[m] iudice[m] p[re]mia
et[er]ne pacis inve[n]iant Amen

    Dat[um] Reate p[er] manu[m] Mag[ist]ri Martini s[an]c[t]e
Romane eccl[es]ie vicecancellarii viij id[us] Maii Indic[cione] ja
Incarnac[i]o[n]is d[omi]nice Anno Mo CCo xxviijo Pontificat[us]
v[er]o d[omi]ni Gregorii P[a]p[e] viiij Anno secundo

Papal Bull of Pope Gregory IX
(Translation, English)

    Bishop Gregory, servant of the servants of God, to his beloved daughters in Christ, the Prioress of the Monastery of Thicket, of the Cistercian order, and her sisters, both present and future, prudent maidens professed to a life according to rule in perpetuity, who in the habit of religion, with torches lit by works of holiness, prepare themselves jointly to go by way of one betrothed.

    The Apostolic See owes protection to be bestowed lest by chance an effort of any temerity whatsoever may either recall them from that purpose or, sacred religion being absent, may weaken a stronghold.

    For that reason we acknowledge to our beloved daughter in Christ that we have kindly assented to your just requests, and to those of your Monastery of Thicket, in which you are entitled to perform divine service under the protection of the Blessed Peter and ourselves, and by the privilege of this present writing we reinforce,

    Establishing in the first place, since it is decreed that the monastic order which follows God and the rule of the Blessed Benedict and the institution of Cistercian Brothers is to be instituted in the same monastery, it shall be inviolably observed in the same place for all time in perpetuity.

    Moreover, whatsoever possessions and goods the same monastery may possess, justly and canonically, at the present time or in the future, by the grant of pontiffs, the generosity of kings or princes, the oblation of the faithful, or by any just means, serving the Lord, may be retained by it, and they may remain, firm and unimpaired, with you and those who succeed you,

Among which we have decided to express these things in our own words; the place itself in which the aforenamed monastery is sited, with all its appurtenances, with its meadows, lands, vineyards, woodlands, wineries and feedings, its woods and open places, its waters and mills, its roads and footpaths, and all its other liberties and immunities;

Indeed, none should presume to exact or extort tithes from you, from possessions of your labours had before this general advice, and also of newly tilled land which was cultivated by your own hands, or at your own costs, or from your gardens, copses and fisheries, or from foodstuffs of your animals.

Also it may be lawful for you etc.

Moreover we confirm, and by the privilege of this present writing reinforce, all liberties and immunities granted to your order by our predecessor Roman Pontiffs, and indeed liberties and exemptions from secular exactions granted by kings and princes, or by other faithful people, inviolably to you, and indults granted by Apostolic authority.

We therefore decree that to no man at all shall it be lawful heedlessly to disturb the aforenamed monastery, or carry away its possessions, or to retain any so carried away, or to weary or harass it with any vexations whatsoever,

But all of those things should be preserved entire, for the governance and sustenance of those to whom they were granted, to all manner of uses for the future, saving the authority of the Apostolic See,

If therefore any person in the future, ecclesiastical or secular, knowing of this deed of our constitution, having been warned, shall heedlessly attempt to go against it for a second or third time, unless he shall have corrected his guilt with fitting satisfaction, let him lose the dignity of his power and honour, and know that he is subject to divine justice; let him acknowledge the injury perpetrated, and let him be estranged from the most sacred body and blood of God and our Lord and redeemer Jesus Christ; and in the final judgment let him undergo severe vengeance.

Moreover, for all those preserving their rights in the same place, may there be the peace of our Lord Jesus Christ, so that they may here receive the fruit of their good deed, and before their righteous judge find the reward of eternal peace, Amen.

Given at Rieti by the hand of Master Martin, Vicechancellor of the Holy Roman Church, on the 8th ides of May, in the 1st indiction, in the 1228th year of the dominical incarnation, and indeed in the second year of the pontificate of our Lord Pope Gregory IX.

Unfortunately, there is no record of the outcome of this dispute, although in all subsequent correspondence between the Archbishop of York and Thicket, the archbishop always refers to them as being of the 'order' of St. Benedict, though that alone does not preclude Thicket from having won their case.

The people that Thicket Priory came into contact with the most were the local people of West Cottingwith, Thorganby and Wheldrake, who were primarily involved in agriculture, mainly as agricultural labourers, some of whom would have worked for the nuns on their demesne lands. Others, further up the social scale, would have been tenants of the nuns on their other land holdings, or as agents of Thicket for those holdings. Unfortunately, the names of the labourers working for the nuns, or the agents, are seldom recorded, and those that were have already been identified in the Servants section of the Internal Community chapter.

Occasionally, the nuns would come into contact with local merchants in their parler, where they could buy provisions and other needed goods, or sell their ale, wool, and other produce from their demesne lands that were surplus to requirements, but no names have been forthcoming.

The only local people that were named from time to time were the families from the upper end of the social spectrum. This included the patrons of Thicket Priory, which as we have seen in the Foundation and Endowments chapter, were the descendants of the founders, the 'de' Haye family of Aughton; and other local lords. In the lay subsidy of 1301 for the vill of Wheldrake, two local lords are named: Magistro Joanne de Craucumbe, who was assessed at 31s. 6d.; Willelmo Darell, assessed at 8s. 10d.; and the Priorissa de Thickeved, assessed at 9s. 10d.[197] It is interesting that the prioress (or priory) is not assessed in the lists for Thorganby or West Cottingwith,

---

[197] *Yorkshire Lay Subsidy, 30 Edw I (1301)*, YASRS 21, p. 106

which would appear that, for tax purposes, the domicile of Thicket was regarded as Wheldrake.

The manor of Aughton continued in the Haye family until the end of the fourteenth century, when German Haye married Alice de Aske, daughter of John de Aske and Joan de Shelvestrode. German died without issue and Alice, his widow, remarried a Thomas Miton (Myton). By some mechanism the manor of Aughton was carried by Alice to her new husband, Thomas Myton. This is unusual, as normally if German had died without issue it would have descended to another in the male line of the Hayes, rather than be carried out of the family on remarriage. Certainly the Haye family felt aggrieved, and Roger Haye petitioned the king:

"Roger Hay states that he was seised of the manors of Aughton and Everthorpe in Yorkshire in his demesne as in fee, until Alice, widow of Thomas Myton, disseised him through the maintenance of her brother, John Ask. He asks the king to order Alice to come before him to be examined on this, and that he might be restored to possession of his manors."[198]

TNA states that this petition is roughly datable to *c.* 1380x1415 by the hand, but is certainly later, as in both 1406 and 1420 the manor was described as belonging to Thomas Myton.[199]

The petition was successful in that it resulted in a legal case being brought in Chancery, Rex v. Milton, in 1434.[200]

It would appear that this suit was unsuccessful, as following Alice's death in 1440 we find John Aske's son, Richard Aske, in possession of the manor.[201] John Aske died 2 June 1429. His son and heir, Richard Aske, was aged 10 and over at his father's death.[202]

In 1531 Sir Robert Aske died, and in his *Inquisition Post Mortem* (IPM) he is stated to hold the Manor of Aughton, the patronage of Ellerton Priory, land and rent in West Cottingwith, Bellasize, Bennetland, and in several other places. His son and heir was John Aske, aged over 30 years. The IPM also

---

[198] TNA, Ref: Ancient Petitions, SC 8/191/9519
[199] *Yorkshire Inquisitions*, YASRS 59, pages 48 and 161
[200] TNA, Ref: C 44/27/7
[201] *Testamenta Eboracensia*, vol. 2, p. 76
[202] 45th Report of the Deputy Keeper of the Public Records, p. 155

recited grants to his second son, Christopher Aske.[203]

Sir Robert had three sons and four daughters, John and Christopher were two of the sons, mentioned in the IPM, and the third and youngest was Robert Aske, leader of the famous Pilgrimage of Grace.[204] Following Robert's execution for his part in the insurrection in July 1537, and the completion of the Dissolution of the Monasteries in 1539, the eldest brother, John, did very well out of the whole affair, acquiring the site and lands of the priories of Marrick, Thicket and Ellerton, in fee, in 1542, in exchange for his manors and land in Sussex.[205]

Throughout all this period, from the marriage of German Haye to Alice de Aske at the end of the fourteenth century to the dissolution of Thicket Priory, the Aske family had been the patrons of Thicket Priory, but just how much of the repairs, improvements and enlargements of the site of the priory the Aske family paid for are simply not recorded.

[203] Hull History Centre, Papers of the Aske Family, Ref: DX55/3

[204] Hoyle, pp. 190–191

[205] L&P vol. 17, Grant 283 (8), p. 158; copy at Hull History Centre, Papers of the Aske Family, Ref: DX55/10

CHAPTER 7
Dissolution
Background – Valor Ecclesiasticus – Compendium Compertorum –
Dissolution – Pensions

In England, from 1337 to 1453, many religious houses had already begun a process akin to dissolution due to the Hundred Years War, when so-called alien priories, i.e. monasteries and priories in England, but under a mother house typically in France, were suppressed and their assets sequestrated, to prevent money going overseas. The assets and income of these alien priories went directly to the crown instead, and some were transferred to royal supporters, and some were earmarked for educational uses.[206]

Towards the end of the fifteenth century many bishops were advocating more dissolutions, with the estates and assets being used to fund educational foundations, typically in new colleges in Oxford and Cambridge.

The power and wealth of the greater monasteries, and their propensity to litigate, even among the lesser religious houses, caused a great deal of animosity among the laity in medieval England. A renowned theologian and critic of monasticism, Desiderius Erasmus of Rotterdam, 1466–1536, regularly satirised monasteries as lax, as comfortably worldly, as wasteful of scarce resources and as superstitious. He also advocated that monks and nuns should be brought more directly under episcopal authority.

In Germany in 1521, Martin Luther had published *De Votis Monasticis* (Concerning Monastic Vows), which ventured that monastic life had no basis in scripture, had no useful purpose, and was incompatible with the true essence of Christianity; while in Sweden, Denmark and Switzerland, confiscations of monasteries were gaining pace in the late 1520s, with the spread of Lutheranism.

Back in England, Henry VIII failed in his bid of 1527 to get a declaration of nullity from the Pope regarding his childless marriage to Catherine of Aragon, his brother's widow, and in 1531 had himself declared Supreme Head of the Church of England, and began a series of legislation to firmly

---

[206] Coredon, p. 10

establish his Supremacy.[207]

Late in 1532 Henry secretly married Anne Boleyn, followed by a second wedding service in London on 25 January 1533. Following the death of Archbishop Warhem, Anne proposed Thomas Cranmer as the new Archbishop of Canterbury who was consecrated 30 March 1533. Less than two months later, Cranmer declared the marriage of Henry and Catherine null and void, and five days later, declared the marriage of Henry and Anne valid.

In November 1534, the 'Act of Supremacy' gave the king the title of 'Supreme Head of the Church of England on Earth', and gave the king the power to correct errors in the church and to conduct ecclesiastical visitations. The 'Act of Conditional Restraint of Annates', also passed in 1534, transferred to the king the 'First Fruits and Tenths' that were previously paid to the Pope.[208] In order to facilitate this transfer Commissioners of the Tenth were appointed throughout the country to establish the taxable value of churches and religious houses. The Commissioners conducted their surveys in the spring and summer of 1535 and their reports were collectively known as the *Valor Ecclesiasticus*.[209]

In the same year, Cromwell was authorised to send Visitors to enquire into all the monasteries, abbeys and priories to assess their observances.

For the North of England, Cromwell chose as his Visitors Richard Layton, a secular cleric who held clerkships in Chancery and the Privy Council, and Thomas Legh, a lawyer and diplomat, and they proceeded together during Christmas 1535. The Visitors interviewed individually each member of the religious houses, and their servants, with tales to tell or scores to settle, urging them all to confess to all manner of sexual deviancy and to inform on one another. The Visitors were deeply unpopular.

Following their Visitations the reports they sent back to Cromwell were collectively known as the *Compendium Compertorum*, and although they took all accusations at face value, no matter how exaggerated, it appears they never fabricated evidence directly.

---

[207] Act in Restraint of Appeals (1533); Submission of the Clergy (1534); Act of Supremacy (1534)

[208] Previously the clergy had to pay a portion of their first year's income (known as annates) to the Pope, and a tenth of their revenue annually thereafter

[209] TNA, Ref: Notes to the class E 344

Parliament met on 4 February 1535/36 and received digests of the *Valor Ecclesiasticus* and the *Compendium Compertorum*, and soon after passed the 'Act for the Dissolution of the Lesser Monasteries', commonly known as the 'Suppression Act', which were defined as those in the *Valor Ecclesiasticus* as having a clear annual income under £200. The above stages will now be discussed, as they applied to Thicket Priory.

The return for Thicket in the *Valor Ecclesiasticus* shows that the clear annual value of the priory was the second smallest of the East Riding nunneries, at only £20 8s. 10d. (only Nunburnholme was smaller). The valuation also listed some rents whose origin have yet to be identified, viz.: 6s. in Lepton;[210] 2s. 6d. in Cliff; 6s. in Spaldington; 10s. in Allerthorpe; 42s. 4d. in Bennetland; and 10s. in Bellasize (*Bellyce*).

The Outgoings consisted of the rents resolute to the chief lords, which included Sir William Percy, the chief lord, who was the tenant-in-chief of the king, in whose fee Thicket was located; the receiver, Thomas Doune was clerk to Sir William, and was responsible for the collection of all monies;[211] John Aske was the bailiff, who was responsible for ensuring that the lands were managed efficiently. His fee was greater than the two senior positions of chief-lord and receiver combined, suggesting that John Aske was the official who actually did the most work. John Aske was the son and heir of Sir Robert Aske, who died 21 February 1530/31.[212] In the *Inquisition Post Mortem* of Sir Robert, it is stated that he held lands and rents in Goodmanham and West Cottingwith, Bellasize and Benetland, (which descended to him through the marriage of German Haye and Alice de Aske at the end of the fourteenth century).[213] The full entry for Thicket Priory was as follows:[214]

---

[210] Leppington, in the parish of Scrayingham, Ref: *A descriptive catalogue of ancient deeds in the Public Record Office*, vol. 1 (1890), A.291

[211] Thomas Doune was described as 'my brother clerke' in the will of Sir William Percy's sister, Josceline Percy, 1532. YAJ, vol. 1 (1870), p. 140

[212] In his *Inquisition Post Mortem*, Sir Robert Aske held lands and rents in Goodmanham and West Cottingwith, Bellasize and Benetland, which descended to him through the marriage of German Haye and Alice de Aske at the end of the fourteenth century. Thereafter, the Aske family became the patrons of Thicket

[213] The IPM of Robert Aske is not in print, but is summerised in the Papers of the Aske Family in Hull History Centre, Ref: U DX 55/3, dated 17 Mar 1531

Priory of the Nuns of Thickhead, Katherine, Prioress, County of Yorks

Value	£	s.	d.
Site of the priory with gardens, mills, meadows and glebe annexed, with their own hands occupied in the soil.		100	
Manors, townships, etc			
West Cottingwith	4	15	10
Thorganby		20	
Sutton upon Derwent		14	6
Youlton		6	
Norton		42	
Lepton (Leppington)		6	
Sand Hutton		60	
Greenhammerton		10	
Cliff		2	6
Osgodby		5	
Escrick		36	
Spaldington		6	
Allerthorpe		10	
City of York		6	
Bennetland		42	4
Bellasize		10	
Total	**23**	**12**	**2**

Outgoings	£	s.	d.
Fee of William Percy, chief-lord		20	
Fee of Thomas Doune, receiver		6	8
Fee of John Aske, bailiff		26	8
Total		**53**	**4**

Clear Value	**20**	**8**	**10**

It is also noticeable that there is no *Spiritualia* for Thicket. They owned no churches, no advowsons, no tithes, and no other spiritual dues or oblations.

The Visitors entered Yorkshire in early January 1536, and were with the

---

[214] TNA, Ref: E 344/21/7; printed in *Valor Ecclesiasticus*, p. 94

Archbishop of York at Cawood 11 January. It was the practice of the Visitors not to visit every religious house at the site of the house, but to send letters in advance requesting the monks and nuns of each house to assemble and meet at some convenient location. Several houses, including Thicket, all within a ten mile radius of York, were examined while the Visitors were at York, and which they completed before 19 January.[215] By the end of February 1536 the Visitation of the Northern Province was over, and Leyton and Legh returned to London.[216] The report from the Visitors for Thicket in the *Compendium Compertorum* was brief: [217]

Matilda Chapman petit dimitti a jugo religionis.
Fundator Johannes Aske
Reddit annuus xxiii[l]

Matilda Chapman seeks release from the yoke of religion.
Founder[218] John Aske
Annual Rents £23

John Aske was the current patron of Thicket Priory, a title which had descended to him through the former estates of the Haye family, which passed to the Aske family through the childless marriage of German Hay and Alice de Aske at the end of the fourteenth century;[219] and before that had descended

---

[215] Shaw, Anthony N., *The Compendium Compertorum and the making of the Suppression Act of 1536*, PhD thesis, Warwick University, (April 2003). The Yorkshire itinerary, with a route map, is given at pp. 201–240, and Thicket at p. 209. The thesis is available online: http://wrap.warwick.ac.uk/1262/1/WRAP_THESIS_Shaw_2003.pdf

[216] *ibid.*, p. 240

[217] L&P, Hen III, vol. X, no. 364, p. 142. This calendar simply says '1 nun seeks release', but the actual manuscript at TNA, Ref: SP 1/102 fol. 97 states explicitly that it is Matilda Chapman who is wishing to be released, *Matilda Chapman petunt dimitti a jugo religionis.*

[218] The translation of *fundator* is 'founder', but in this context the reports are referring to the current patron

[219] But this was subject to a petition to the king by a member of the Hay family: "Roger Hay states that he was seised of the manors of Aughton and Everthorpe in Yorkshire in his demesne as in fee, until Alice, widow of Thomas Myton, disseised him through the

from the actual founder, Roger son of Roger, to his sister Emma, who married Roger Hay, as we have seen in the Foundation and Endowments chapter.

Following the *Valor Ecclesiasticus* and the *Compendium Compertorum,* the 'Suppression of Religious Houses Act' or the 'Act for the Dissolution of the Lesser Monasteries', as it was known, was passed by Parliament in February 1535/6. However, Clause XIII of the Act stated the following:

> XIII Provided always, that the king's highness, at any time after the making of this act, may at his pleasure ordain and declare, by his letters patents under his great seal, that such of the said religious houses which his highness shall not be disposed to have suppressed nor dissolved by authority of this act, shall still continue, remain, and be in the same body corporate, and in the said essential estate, quality, and condition, as well in possessions as otherwise, as they were afore the making of this Act…[220]

The Act also provided for the appointment of local Commissioners or Particular Receivers to visit the houses under the £200 threshold and report back. The Articles for these Commissioners required them to establish their authority over each head of each religious house by exhibiting the Act, and swear them to answer all their questions fully and honestly. The Commissioners were to undertake an inventory of all immovable assets (lands and buildings, etc.), and movable assets (plate, jewels, bells, money, furniture, farming stock and other goods). They were then required to question each member of the religious house as to whether they wished to be moved to another house of the same order, or to return to the secular life with a pension. The Commissioners then took possession of the seal of the house, together with all plate, jewels and money, to be kept 'in a safe place', and commanded

---

maintenance of her brother, John Ask. He asks the King to order Alice to come before him to be examined on this, and that he might be restored to possession of his manors." (TNA, Ref: Ancient Petitions, SC 8/191/9519). The petition was successful in that it resulted in a legal case being brought in Chancery, Rex v. Milton , in 1434, TNA, Ref: C 44/27/7, but it would appear that this suit was unsuccessful, as following Alice's death in 1440 we find John Aske's son, Richard Aske, in possession of the manor. John Aske died 2 June 1429. His son and heir, Richard Aske, was aged 10 and over at his father's death

[220] Statutes of the Realm, iii, p. 577

each house to continue tilling and sowing until the king's pleasure be known.[221] The Commissioners then sent all this information on each house back to London and to await further instructions.

After analysis of these Commissioner's Reports or 'brief certificates' some thirty-three religious houses in Yorkshire were found to be liable to be suppressed, being under the £200 clear annual value threshold, but only fifteen houses of this total of were immediately suppressed. These fifteen had all their movables sold, save the plate, jewels and money, and their heads sent to the alternative houses of their choice, and the rest to the Archbishop of Canterbury or the Lord Chancellor to learn their 'capacities' (rewards for surrendering). That left eighteen to survive. Seven of these eighteen were granted Letters Patent of exemption, in accordance with the above Clause XIII of the Act,[222] and a further three had 'special' status.[223] That left eight houses that had no formal or 'special' exemption. These were Basedale, Esholt, Grosmont, Handale, Thicket, Wilberfoss, Wykeham and Yeddingham.

When all these eight were finally dissolved along with the greater monasteries in 1539 the reason given was to be compliant with the earlier 'Suppression of Religious Houses Act' of 1536. The seven who were granted Letters Patent were treated specifically within the 1539 Act, showing that the eight that had survived up to that Act had no formal status.

The reason why the eight houses, including Thicket, survived the first 1536 Act has been explored by Woodward,[224] who found that the local Particular Receivers mainly responsible for the Yorkshire suppressions, Leonard

---

[221] No list of the plate, jewels, bells etc. of Thicket is known to exist. It is known that they did have, at least, a communion cup, worth 4½ marks for their chapel, granted by King Henry III in January 1252, CLR, vol. 4, p. 16; and nine foot torches, left to Thicket in the will of John Croxton of York in March 1393, York Minster Archives, Ref: CY/ZC/L/2/4 f. 111

[222] L&P, xi, 385 (34); 1417 (13); xii, part 2, 1008 (2); xiii, part 1, 646 (17); 646 (18); 1115 (19); 1519 (44). Alphabetically: Arthington; Hampole; Kirklees, Nunappleton; Nunkeeling; St. Michael's Priory, Hull; and Swine

[223] The Gilbertine houses of Ellerton, Malton and St. Andrew's, York, survived, as the head of their order, Robert Holgate, had great influence with Cromwell. Holgate was to become Bishop of Llandaff (1537), President of the Council in the North (1538), and Archbishop of York (1545)

[224] Woodward, pp. 385–401

Beckwith and Hugh Fuller, had a set of instructions which contained the following intriguing sentence, which he believed concerned the above eight houses, 'which our sovereign lord the king hath promised to continue with t... religious persons of them still yet remaining in...without any confirmation or establishment by the King's letters p...thereof made'. [225] This document suggests that the king had made verbal promises to the eight, but for some reason had never issued formal Letters Patent.

When all the remaining Greater and Lesser Monasteries had finally been persuaded (or intimidated) by the Commissioners to surrender throughout 1537–1539, the final 'Act for the Dissolution of Abbeys' was passed in the autumn of 1539, which simply ratified what the Particular Receivers had managed to accomplish. [226] The eight surviving lesser houses in Yorkshire were not mentioned, as they were still under the provisions of the earlier 1536 Act, and their suppression had been simply completed before the 1539 Act.

Thicket Priory was one of the last to be surrendered, being surrendered by the prioress, Agnes Beckwith, on the 27 August 1539. [227]

Following the surrender of Thicket Priory the immovable assets were listed and entered in the List of the lands of Dissolved Religious Houses, which was one category of entries in the List of Ministers' Accounts. The list was made from the earliest account available following the surrender, and in the case of Thicket Priory it was the first account. Rents from the immovable assets were:

Farm[228] of the site of the priory and demesne lands, with a mill.

Rents and farms in Westcotyngwithe, Benett Lande, Belyces, Alkerthorpe, Thorgunbye, Sutton upon Dervent, Lepyngton, Norton, Sandhutton (including a tenement or manor), Grene Hamerton, in Copergate and without Mikilgate in the City of York, Yotton, Osgodbye, Cliff, Escreyke, Bowton, Draxe by Clyff, Wheldrik and Spawdyngton.[229]

---

[225] *ibid.*, p. 391

[226] *Statutes of the Realm*, iii, p. 733–9. This act did not, in fact, dissolve any houses but simply ratified what the commissioners had managed to do by persuasion and intimidation

[227] Yorkshire Monasteries Suppression Papers, YASRS vol. 48, (1912), p. 161

[228] In this context, the word 'farm' means 'the lease of' or 'the rental of'

[229] TNA, Ref: SC 6/HenVIII/4522

As can be seen, the property owned by the priory generating rental income loosely matches that of the list in the *Valor Ecclesiasticus* above, but gives a little more detail. It specifies the areas where their property lay in the City of York, and additionally gives land holdings in Bowton, [230] Drax and Wheldrake.

Only the heads of houses (*i.e.* abbots, priors or prioresses) were offered pensions in 1536 if they voluntarily surrendered. However, in the case of nunneries it soon became very clear to the commissioners that the nuns had no other religious avenue open to them, other than going to another nunnery,[231] but as no nunnery in the country had a clear annual value of over £200 then dispersal to other houses was simply not possible. Consequently, all later surrenders of nunneries were conditional upon all the nuns receiving a pension, and so it was with Thicket Priory.

Following the dissolution of Thicket in 1539, each of the nuns was granted a 'reward' and a pension. However, as can be seen from the following two lists, the pension of the last prioress, Agnes Beckwith, was the subject of some revision, rising from an initial pension of 53s. 4d. offered by the commissioners in 1536, to an increased pension of 56s. 8d. at the dissolution of Thicket in 1539, then to £6 13s. 4d. when the pension granted was enrolled in the Court of Augmentations. None of the other nuns had their pensions revised in this way.

Could Agnes Beckwith, and the Receiver, Leonard Beckwith, be related? It certainly looks like someone influential was lobbying on behalf of Agnes.

---

[230] Possibly Bolton, in the parish of Bishop Wilton, two miles north-west of Pocklington

[231] Monks had various options open to them. They could join the regular clergy, or become chaplains, or the heads of religious fraternities, etc. None of these options were available to nuns

Pensions in 1539[232]

Name	Pension		Reward
Agnes Beckwith, prioress	53s. 4d. (struck out) 56s. 8d. (struck out)		20s.
Alicia Yonge	33s. 4d.		13s. 4d.
Margaret Kychynman	26s. 8d.		10s.
Elena Sterkey	26s. 8d.		10s.
Matilda Chapman	20s.		10s.
Agnes Hunsley	20s.		10s.
Margaret Swale	20s.		10s.
Isabella Cawton	20s.		10s.
Elena Fisher	20s.		10s.

Pensions Enrolled in the Augmentation Books 1539–40[233]

Name	Pension
Agnes Beckwith, prioress	£6 13s. 4d.
Alicia Yonge	33s. 4d.
Margaret Kychynman	26s. 8d.
Elena Sterkey	26s. 8d.
Matilda Chapman	20s.
Agnes Hunsley	20s.
Margaret Swale	20s.
Isabella Cawton	20s.
Elena Fisher	20s.

Most, if not all, simply returned to secular life, with some marrying and some going back to live with their families. We simply do not know, as their

---

[232] TNA, Ref: SP 5/2 fols. 48 (pensions), 55 (rewards); printed in YASRS vol. 80, Miscellanea, vol. III, A Selection of Monastic Rentals and Dissolution Papers (1931), pp. 87–90

[233] TNA, Ref: Augmentation Books, vol. 234, fol. 268b; printed in L&P, vol. xv, p. 551; and in YASRS vol. 48, *Yorkshire Monasteries, Suppression Papers*, (1912), p. 161

names vanish from the public record, except in the records of their pension receipts.

Pension Lists to 1582

Name	Pension	1553 List	1556 List	1564 List	1582 List
Agnes Beckwith	£6 13s. 4d.	✓	✓	✓	
Alice Yong	33s. 4d.				
Margaret Kytchynman	26s. 8d.	✓	✓		
Ellen Starkye	26s. 8d.	✓	✓	✓	✓
Matilda Chapman	20s.	✓	✓	✓	✓
Agnes Hunsley	20s.	✓	✓	✓	
Marjory Swale	20s.	✓	✓	✓	✓
Isabella Cawton	20s.	✓	✓	✓	
Ellen Fyssher	20s.	✓	✓		

Lists of the surviving pensioners of Thicket exist for 1552/3, 1556, 1564 and 1582. Of the nine original pensioners in 1539, eight were still drawing their pension in 1553 and 1556, six in 1564, and just three in 1582: Ellen Starkey; Matilda Chapman; and Marjory Swale, who were now all aged in their seventies.[234]

Thicket Priory had survived for over 350 years, and its last nun would have died over 400 years since its foundation, but she was not to be the last nun to reside at Thicket.

The subsequent history of the site of Thicket Priory is contained in the second booklet in the series, *Thicket Priory, Dissolution to Thicket Priory II*. The story of Thicket Priory III and the nuns who once again made their home there, is contained in the third and last booklet in the series, *Thicket Priory, Rebirth and the Return of the Nuns*.

Colin Blanshard Withers

---

[234] TNA, Ref: E 101/76/23 (1553); E 164/3 fol. 57 (1556); LR 6/122/8 m. 23 (1564); LR 6/122/9 m. 20 (1582)